| DATE DUE | | | |
|---|---|---|---|
|  |  |  |  |
|  |  |  |  |
|  |  |  |  |
|  |  |  |  |
|  |  |  |  |
|  |  |  |  |
|  |  |  |  |
|  |  |  |  |
|  |  |  |  |
|  |  |  |  |
|  |  |  |  |

HENRY STEELE COMMAGER'S

# AMERICANS

# ANDREW JACKSON
## *and the New Populism*

BY WILLIAM GUTMAN

Illustrations by Rodger Xavier

CHILDRENS PRESS CHOICE

A Barron's title selected for educational distribution

ISBN 0-516-08585-9

92 6527

First edition published 1987
by Barron's Educational Series, Inc.

All inquiries should be addressed to:
Barron's Educational Series, Inc.
250 Wireless Blvd.
Hauppauge, NY 11788

Library of Congress Catalog No. 87-72376

International Standard Book No. 0-8120-3917-3

*Printed in the United States of America*
7 8 9 0    9 6 9 3    9 8 7 6 5 4 3 2 1

# CONTENTS

*Introduction*                                           v

**Chapter 1**
Meet Andrew Jackson                                      1

**Chapter 2**
Young Andrew                                             6

**Chapter 3**
Revolution Comes Home                                    16

**Chapter 4**
Prisoner of War                                          32

**Chapter 5**
A Surprise Inheritance                                   42

**Chapter 6**
The Wanderer                                             49

**Chapter 7**
Lawyer, Landowner, Husband                               58

**Chapter 8**
A Busy Life                                              70

**Chapter 9**
The War Years                                            88

**Chapter 10**
The Battle of New Orleans                                109

**Chapter 11**
Private Life, But Not For Long                           126

**Chapter 12**
Triumph and Tragedy                                      137

# CONTENTS

**Chapter 13**
    Mr. President     145

*Glossary*     161
*Topics for Discussion*     163
*Reference Book List*     165
*Map Activity*     166
*Index*     168

Andrew Jackson was just a boy when the American Revolution broke out, but he managed to join the fight at the Battle of Hanging Rock where his brother was killed and he was wounded. A natural soldier and leader, he fought the British again in the War of 1812 and, at the Battle of New Orleans, gave them the worst defeat they had suffered in three hundred years.

He fought not only the British, but the Indians and the Spanish, too. The Indians he ousted from their tribal lands, the Spanish from the Florida territory. While fighting in Florida, he almost got the United States involved in another war with England by hanging two Englishmen whom he accused of stirring up the Indians.

Besides doing all of this fighting, he served his country as a politician, as well. He was a congressman, a senator, a judge, and in 1828 he became president. Six presidents had preceded him, but in one sense he was the first "American" president—the first "Man of the People." Born in poverty, he had fought his way to wealth, but never forgot what it had been like to be poor and powerless. Unlike Washington, Jefferson and the Adamses, he had no ancestors to boast about. He had no formal education, but then, neither had George Washington; like Washington, he managed pretty well.

As president, he no longer fought with weapons, but the battles continued. He fought constitutional battles with John Marshall and Joseph Story of the Supreme Court. He fought political battles with Daniel Webster and John C. Calhoun (whom he threatened to hang if he persisted in trying to nullify national laws). He fought political and financial battles with the president of the Bank of the United States, which he wanted to abolish. In the end he usually had his way. He saw himself as the representative, not of any one section of the country, but of all the people, and he was indeed. He was not venerated like Washington, or esteemed like Jefferson and Madison, but he was idolized by his followers. No wonder, since he changed traditional political habits by filling national offices with trusted supporters. Even the judiciary was chosen on partisan lines, with the president expecting that judges would do his bidding. All this shocked the respectable statesmen who had controlled American politics since the Inauguration of Washington, but it pleased the people. For better or for worse, Jackson became the model of the modern American president.

Henry Steele Commager
*Amherst, Massachusetts*

# CHAPTER ONE

# Meet Andrew Jackson

The British officer looked closely at the fourteen-year-old boy standing before him. He had expected the youngster to be frightened. After all, the boy was about to become a prisoner of war. Yet he stood his ground and stared back at the officer. Finally, the officer gave the boy a command.

"Clean my boots," he said.

For young Andrew Jackson, it was perhaps the first real moment of truth in his life. Though he didn't know it then, he would face many more such moments. How he reacted here would set the tone for the years to come.

"No, get someone else to clean them!"

"What!" The officer couldn't believe his ears.

"Get someone else. I am a prisoner of war, not your servant."

The Briton was furious. How dare a colonial boy refuse the command of an officer in the British army? He drew back his sword and swung it violently at the boy's head!

Young Andrew threw up his left arm. The sword cut his wrist to the bone and put a nasty gash in his head.

*The British officer swung his sword violently at the boy's head.*

The boy was stunned and bleeding. He would carry scars of those wounds for the rest of his life. Yet it wasn't the end of his troubles. Soon after that, still bruised and weakened, Andrew Jackson was forced to march forty miles without food or water to the place where he would be held prisoner.

Though it may sound shocking that a fourteen-year-old boy could be a prisoner of the mighty British army, it was not unusual. The year was 1781, and there was a great struggle taking place. The American colonists were fighting for their independence from England. Many brave teenagers wanted to fight in what one day would be known as the American Revolutionary War.

Andrew Jackson was one of those young men. When his older brother died after the battle of Stone Ferry, he felt he had to take action. The war was now a threat to his home and family, as well as to his freedom. Despite his young age, he was ready to risk his life for home and country.

The Americans won their independence from England. But the youthful Jackson paid a huge price. He lost both his brothers and his beloved mother to the war. His father had died years earlier, shortly before Andrew was born.

As a boy entering his teens, Andrew was suddenly without an immediate family. Though he still had his extended family (aunts, uncles, and cousins) nearby, it wasn't quite the same. With no one to guide him, he might have simply disappeared into the American frontier, never to be heard from again. If he had done that, America would not be the same nation it is today.

Andrew Jackson did not take the easy way out. After he recovered from his shattering losses, he decided to make something of his life. He went on to achieve what most people only dream of. He would grow up to become the most popular American of his time. And though he never wanted a life in politics, he never turned his back on his country, either.

In 1828, the same young boy who was cut by the

British officer's sword was elected the seventh president of the United States.

In many ways, he was an unlikely choice. He was the first of the "log cabin" presidents: men born and raised on the frontier, the rough and tumble fringes of a growing country. The first six presidents had all come from the traditional areas of culture and schooling, Virginia and New England.

Jackson was an outsider, a man considered crude and even violent by many politicians. But in a rapidly changing America, he was the people's choice and the first real people's president. Tall and straight, with a shock of thick, white hair, he cut a bold figure. He was tough and quick, a valuable friend and feared enemy. He was a man you did not double-cross.

By the time he entered the White House, he had already lived a full life, having experienced his share of both triumph and tragedy. Two severe bullet wounds and serious trouble with money threatened to destroy him. Finally, his beautiful wife died the night before he took office as president. But a will of iron got him through even the worst of times.

"I know what I am fit for," Andrew Jackson once said. "I can command a body of men in a rough way; but I am not fit to be president."

How wrong he was. In his own way, he was perfectly fit to be president. He was a man for his time, pulling together a growing young nation with a firm hand. And if there was one thing the man called "Old Hickory" had, it was a firm hand.

From a youngster on the Carolina frontier to a teen-ager defying the British, from victorious general to president of the nation, Andrew Jackson's life was an American adventure. Surprisingly enough, Andrew Jackson's story did not begin in America, but in a place called Carrickfergus, in Northern Ireland.

# CHAPTER TWO

# Young Andrew

Andrew Jackson's forefathers had originally come to Carrickfergus from Scotland. His grandfather, Hugh Jackson, was a successful linen weaver and merchant, who had his own store. But his father, also named Andrew Jackson, had turned to farming out of love for the land. As a young man, Andrew's father married the red-haired Elizabeth Hutchinson, whose family had also come from Scotland. Together, they started a small farm and set out to raise a family.

By the early spring of 1765, the Jacksons already had two sons. Hugh was two years old and little Robert just five months. But Mr. Jackson wasn't happy. Though he worked very hard at farming the land, the rewards were small.

Because of the laws in Carrickfergus, Mr. Jackson wasn't allowed to own the land he farmed. Instead, he had to pay rent, and that took away the profit from his farming. More than anything else, Andrew Jackson wanted his own land. At last, he made a courageous decision. Mr. Jackson decided to follow a number of his relatives and sail across the great Atlantic Ocean to seek a new life in America.

The Jacksons left Ireland in April of 1765, with their two young sons and a few personal belongings. The ocean voyage was long and hard. The wooden sailing ship was small and cramped. With its three masts and billowy white canvas sails, it was often tossed about by strong winds and heavy seas. There were times when Andrew and Elizabeth wondered if they would ever see land again. But their spirits were kept up by their hopes and dreams for the future.

They landed near Philadelphia, Pennsylvania, in May. But that was only their first stop. A number of their relatives, including several of Mrs. Jackson's sisters, had traveled some five hundred miles west by wagon. They had settled in a frontier area known as the Waxhaws, close to the border between North and South Carolina.

The journey west by wagon was difficult and sometimes dangerous. The wagons bounced and pitched over the bumpy, rough-cut roads. Wheels fell off sometimes and the men would have to repair them. If they were beyond repair, the wagons would have to be left behind. The further west the Jacksons went, the harder it was. Roads grew even worse. The thick woods and forests were full of insects and mosquitoes.

At night, the settlers slept under the wagons. If it rained, their possessions got wet and only the sun could dry things out. Food supplies ran low. The men couldn't always hunt because of the threat of hostile Indians. Many turned back. Others became weak and ill, and several died. Those who completed the journey knew it was not an easy life which lay ahead.

They were in frontier country, where people and houses were a rare sight. The land had to be cleared and tilled, houses built, roads cut, stores opened. Everyone moving to the frontier had to start their lives over again. But after traveling hundreds of miles to find new homes, the settlers were all eager to make the most of it.

The Jackson family settled in the Waxhaws. Mr. Jackson took to working very hard, as did all the settlers in the area. The older settlers welcomed new people to the region. They all tried to get along as best they could with the Indians who lived nearby. With many friends and family so close and all working together, the Jacksons were happy and hopeful. In February of 1767, Mrs. Jackson was about a month away from bearing her third child. It would be her first born in America. Then tragedy struck.

While trying to lift a very heavy log, Mr. Jackson hurt himself badly. He was put to bed in great pain. There were few doctors on the frontier then. Medical knowledge was limited. His family and friends tried to make Mr. Jackson comfortable, but they could do no more. Within several days he was dead.

Grief-stricken, Elizabeth Jackson tried to go on with her life. She went to live with her sister and brother-in-law, Jane and James Crawford, on a nearby farm. On March 15, her third son was born. She named him Andrew after her husband, the father he would never know.

Elizabeth Jackson and her children continued to live

with the Crawfords. Fortunately, there were many other family members nearby to help them cope with their tragic loss. It wasn't unusual to find large families living close together on the frontier. Often there were parents and grandparents, children, uncles, aunts, and cousins, all living within a few miles of each other. These extended families worked together, always lending a hand to both family and neighbor. There were people to take care of every task. The men who were the best carpenters built the houses. Those who were crack shots did the hunting. Others helped make the roads.

The women would make and mend the clothing, and prepare and preserve the food. They also cared for the children.

Since Elizabeth Jackson's ancestors had been weavers, she was very familiar with the craft. She took to spinning yarn, getting the threads ready to be woven into various articles of clothing—socks, dresses, coats, and even blankets. She worked very hard. The job she did was very important in a frontier community.

It was a busy time in the Waxhaws. James Crawford's farm was growing. Then suddenly, his wife, Jane, who had been weak and ill for several years, died. Elizabeth Jackson took on the running of the house in her sister's place. With extended families, there was always someone ready and willing to fill any gaps in the community or in the family.

Young Andrew's early years in the Waxhaws were peaceful and happy. He was an active youngster who hated to sit still for too long. While it was always a battle

9

to keep him in school at the Waxhaw Church, he learned very quickly and often on his own.

By the time he was five, he could read better than many adults. Besides learning in school, he would pick up every newspaper he could find and read it from front to back. It was a habit that would last a lifetime. At eight, he was writing in script. His mother began to think he was going to be something special. For a time, she thought someday he might even be a preacher.

Andrew continued to grow, both in mind and body. By the time he was nine, he was already a "public reader." Since so many of the settlers couldn't read at all, newspapers that brought word of events back East were read out loud for them.

Though he was dwarfed by the men and women around him, young Andrew would stand up straight in the town meetings and begin to read. In a high-pitched voice, he read the paper right through without stumbling. He was chosen to read as often as any grown man, and that made him proud. It was a real honor to be a public reader in a frontier community.

When he wasn't reading, he was busy playing outdoors. He was a very good horseman at an early age. It didn't matter how wild the animal, Andrew would mount up and take off. He would often ride, as fast as he could, over the fields and hills of the Waxhaws.

If he wasn't riding, he was running and jumping. Young Andrew and his friends loved to run over the Waxhaws. They would jump fences, climb rocks and trees, race, and play games of tag. While he grew tall,

*By the time Andrew was nine, he was already a "public reader."*

Andrew was always thin. The bigger, heavier boys sometimes took advantage of that.

Though he didn't always win the fights he had, he never quit, not once. As one of his early classmates said:

"I could throw him three times out of four, but he would never stay throwed. He was dead game and never would give up."

Andrew was a freckled-faced youngster. He had bright blue eyes and thick, messy hair that was almost red in color. He was known for having a quick temper. If any one of the boys teased him about anything, a fight was not far off. It didn't matter how big or strong the other boy might be.

He also learned to use a musket from the time he was strong enough to lift one. Young boys learned to shoot early on the frontier. A person never knew when they might have to shoot to save their life, or the lives of loved ones.

One time, Andrew's friends gave him a gun that was loaded with more gunpowder than usual. The extra powder gave the gun an extra kick that sent the youngster sprawling to the ground. He didn't stay down long. He leapt to his feet, fists clenched and eyes afire.

"By God," he roared, "if one of you laughs, I'll kill him!"

In 1778, when he was eleven, Andrew took part in a cattle drive. He helped run a herd of cattle from the Waxhaws to Charles Town, the great South Carolina city on the ocean. Since it was his first drive, he had the dif-

*In 1778, on his first cattle drive, Andrew began to feel like a man.*

ficult job of riding in the rear. He was supposed to make
sure there were no stragglers. It was dirty work. He spent
most of his time peering through the thick cloud of dust
that rose up from the cows and horses in front of him.

It was quite a responsibility for an eleven-year-old.
But the men knew he was a good enough rider to handle
the job. Andrew loved living out in the open with the
men, and listening to their stories. In those days, a man
had to be able to live outdoors if he wanted to travel.
And on the cattle drive, Andrew Jackson was beginning
to feel like a man.

Sleeping under the stars didn't bother him, nor did
a couple of soaking rains that left him drenched from head
to foot. There were dangers, too. Cattle can always

stampede without warning, crushing everything in their path. And there was the ever-present worry about Indians. Would they be friendly or hostile?

The cattle drive was a real adventure for a young boy, something right out of the Old West. Andrew was even more amazed when he saw Charles Town, a huge city in those days, with about one thousand people. Young Andrew had never seen real houses and streets before. Instead of rough cabins and dirt trails, the houses of Charles Town were wood frame and brick, the roads paved and flat.

He also fell in love with the harbor. There were large sailing ships docked there, just like the ones his parents had taken when they came to America. The ocean was blue and beautiful. It stretched so far out in front of him that he couldn't see any land, just white-capped water stretching over the far horizon.

Andrew walked the streets of Charles Town with wide-eyed wonder. There were wooden sidewalks and people dressed in fine clothes. The women wore silk dresses and carried parasols to shade them from the sun. The men wore neat broadcloth suits and smoked big cigars. Many of them weren't even carrying guns, something unheard of in the Waxhaws. Elegant horse-drawn carriages were another luxury that didn't exist back home. Yes, Charles Town was a place he definitely wanted to see again.

Once Andrew was back home in the Waxhaws, his mother said she wanted him to return to school.

*Andrew was captivated by the harbor at Charles Town.*

"Do I have to, Ma?" he said. He already considered himself a cowboy.

"You certainly do, Andrew. More schoolin' is the best thing for you right now."

He knew better than to argue with his mother. So he spent some time at the nearby Francis Cummins Boarding School, where he learned Latin as well as the regular readin', writin', and 'rithmetic. He stayed at the school on and off until it closed in early 1780. By then, national events were about to affect everyone in the Waxhaws. And they would change young Andrew Jackson's life forever.

# Revolution Comes Home

The rumblings of war had actually started several years earlier. The American colonists were getting tired of what they considered unfair laws set up by the ruling country, England. Though it sometimes took weeks, even months, for news to reach the Waxhaws, the settlers there knew that something very big was about to happen.

Much of the problem with England stemmed from what the colonists felt were unfair taxes on goods coming in from that country. The unrest began about the time of Andrew's birth in the mid-1760s. The Townshend Acts, a set of laws passed by the British Parliament, in 1767, made the colonists particularly angry.

The Townshend Acts placed a tax on many products coming from England, including lead, glass, paint, paper, wine, and tea. Even worse, the new laws gave British officials the right to search people's houses for those products!

In Philadelphia, New York, and Boston, red-coated British soldiers could be seen going through colonists' stores and banging on the doors of homes at all hours of the day and night. "Time to search," they'd say, and it was all legal. This angered the colonists even more, especially in the large cities on the east coast.

There was so much unrest in Boston that, in 1768, King George of England sent four thousand troops into the city. He also sent out warships, vessels with large cannons protruding from gunports on each side. They looked strong and threatening, sitting in Boston Harbor.

But the sight of the armed British troops only made matters worse. Finally, on March 5, 1770, the powder keg exploded.

Several Boston boys began taunting a British guard. Soon they were throwing snowballs at him as well. The guard called for help. Before long, an entire squad of soldiers, armed with muskets, faced a growing crowd. Angry words were exchanged. Then the crowd began throwing bricks, bottles, and cobblestones at the soldiers.

Suddenly, one of the British soldiers fired his musket into the crowd. The other soldiers followed suit. The crowd started to scatter as the smoke from the volley rose slowly through the cold, gray winter sky. Five colonists lay dead and several others were badly wounded.

News of the shootings traveled rapidly throughout the colonies. The event was quickly labeled the Boston Massacre. Angry feelings towards England grew with each day. Yet the taxation continued. By December of 1773, the citizens of Boston decided that something had to be done.

On the night of December 16, a group of colonists painted their faces and put on headfeathers. Disguised as

Indians, the colonists boarded three British cargo ships in Boston Harbor. The ships were loaded with cases of tea. The colonists dumped every last case of tea on those ships overboard into the water. People in Boston cheered, and news about the "Boston Tea Party" was greeted with joy throughout the colonies.

The British responded by closing Boston Harbor, and the soldiers took over to rule the city. The colonies and England were on a collision course.

In September of 1774, the colonies decided to band together and form a congress. The purpose was to protest England's rule. Delegates to the First Continental Congress met in Philadelphia, and once again asked the British Parliament to stop collecting the unfair taxes.

The delegates also pledged to support the people of Boston. But Boston Harbor remained closed. England wouldn't give an inch. Even the King, George III, recognized that war might not be far off.

"The die is now cast," he said. "The colonies must either submit or triumph."

War was in the air. Though some American colonists, called Tories or Loyalists, were still loyal to Britain, the majority, called Patriots, wanted independence. In the Boston area, some of the Patriots formed a group called the Minutemen. Their name meant they were ready to go to battle with just a minute's notice. General Thomas Gage, leader of the British troops, heard about the Minutemen. He wanted to find out where they were storing their weapons.

The Patriots' storehouse of weapons was in the

small, sleepy town of Concord, Massachusetts, about twenty miles from Boston. On April 18, 1775, Minutemen leaders got word that General Gage and his troops had crossed Boston's Charles River. The British planned a quick march into Concord and nearby Lexington, and were fast approaching. Two Patriots, Paul Revere and William Dawes, mounted their horses and rode all night to warn the Minutemen that the British were coming.

It was early on the morning of April 19 when the British reached Lexington. Less than one hundred Minutemen were waiting for them.

"Look at all them Redcoats," one Minuteman whispered.

"There's just too many," said another. "They'll wipe us out."

The Minutemen began to pull back when the British saw them.

"Fire," yelled a red-coated officer.

Shots rang out in the damp morning air. Minutemen began to fall. The ones that weren't shot retreated. When the smoke cleared, eight Minutemen lay dead. Another ten had been wounded. The brief fight seemed a ridiculously easy triumph for the British. But although it wasn't a real battle, the guns that flared at Lexington marked the beginning of the American Revolution.

While Lexington might have been easy for the British, Concord was not. When the Redcoats got there, the Minutemen were ready for them. They blasted away at the British from behind every rock, tree, wall, house, and hill. This time there were many more of them. Grown

men and young boys helped drive the British back to
Boston, as Minutemen snipers fired at them all the way.

Shortly afterward, some six thousand American soldiers under General Artemas Ward surrounded the city
of Boston. They managed to keep Gage's troops from
leaving. The British knew then that the war would not
be an easy one, nor would it be over quickly. They began
making plans to send more troops and ships to America,
and looked for the best places to land them.

Andrew Jackson's neighbors in the Waxhaws followed events in Boston from the beginning. When the
British closed Boston Harbor following the Tea Party,
the settlers sent corn, barley, and cattle east to help feed
the citizens of Boston. And once they heard of the fighting at Lexington and Concord, the men of the Waxhaws
knew they had to be ready, too.

"What if the British land at Charles Town?" one said.

"They could overrun the whole area in no time at
all," said another.

"Then we can't let them land," said a third.

It was not long before the Waxhaw Militia Company
was formed. Andrew's uncle, Robert Crawford, was
chosen as its captain. In June of 1776, the militia marched
to Charles Town. Sure enough, the colonists heard that
the British were sending ships loaded with troops toward
Charles Town Harbor.

Along with other groups of patriots, the Waxhaw
militia waited in a pasture six miles from the harbor. They
were ready to battle any British troops that made it

ashore. They didn't want the English to take over Charles Town.

Fortunately, the Waxhaw men didn't have to fight. Colonists fired on the British ships with cannons placed in the mouth of the harbor. The colonial gunners were on target. Several ships were hit, and several others got bogged down in the mud. After a short but fierce battle, the British headed back to sea. They would have to find another place to land. It wouldn't be Charles Town Harbor, at least not this time.

Robert Crawford's militia returned to the Waxhaws in July. Then in August, some astonishing news reached the settlement. The news came via month-old newspapers from Philadelphia. People came to Robert Crawford's from miles around to hear it. The reader was nine-year-old Andrew Jackson. With family, friends, neighbors, and many strangers gathered around him, Andrew began. He carefully pronounced even the most difficult words.

" '*In Congress, July 4, 1776,*" he began. "*The Unanimous Declaration of the Thirteen United States of America.*' "

He paused, letting the people digest the words, then continued.

" '*When in the Course of human events, it becomes necessary for one people to dissolve the political bands which have connected them with another . . .*' "

Andrew continued reading right through to the end. When he finished, the crowd was buzzing with excitement. It was the most astonishing piece of news that had ever come to the Waxhaws. Even young Andrew could hardly believe what he had just read. It was a Declaration of Independence.

"You mean we're a country now?" one man asked. "No more listening to them redcoats?"

"It means we're a free country, all right," said another. "But we're gonna have to prove it to the British. And you know how we got to do that."

"With guns."

"Yeah, send 'em back across that ocean."

"Don't worry, we'll lick 'em."

The Declaration of Independence gave new meaning to the war. Yet after the British attempt to land in Charles Town in early 1776, the Waxhaws saw very little fighting for nearly three years. The main war was taking place in the Northeast. Newspapers brought accounts of victories and defeats, and of new American heroes like General George Washington. But life in the Waxhaws went on pretty much as usual.

Andrew Jackson grew and matured. He learned to shoot well and became an excellent rider. He had a happy childhood. But news of the war continued to come with newspapers and visitors. Andrew was well aware of events, since he was the public reader. He studied every newspaper that came into town.

Pretty soon it was more than just newspaper stories. By early 1780, the British had sent troops to the South. This time they were more successful. They overran Georgia and began marching through South Carolina. Once again, Robert Crawford's militia got the call. This time

Andrew's older brother, Hugh, who was then sixteen, joined them.

At a place called Stone Ferry, the first major battle was fought. Once again the Americans stopped the British, forcing them to retreat to Georgia. But now the Jackson family felt the full effect of the war. Hugh Jackson had fallen ill before the battle. He was ordered not to fight. But he was a Jackson, and that meant he would not say no to his duty. He fought despite his illness.

When the battle was over, Hugh Jackson collapsed. Nothing could be done to help him, and a short time later he was dead. Andrew, his mother, and brother Robert all grieved at Hugh's death. The war was coming to the Waxhaws. In a very short time, it would involve them all.

Now that they had a foothold in the South, the British kept attacking. Another fleet sailed into Charles Town Harbor. This time the British troops made it ashore. On May 12, 1780, the redcoats captured Charles Town and took many American prisoners, including Andrew's uncle, Robert Crawford.

He was later set free when he promised not to fight again. But as soon as he was back home he reorganized the militia, along with Colonel Thomas Sumter. The Patriots had another worry now. There was a newly organized band of British supporters in the area. Now that the British troops had appeared in the area to protect them, these "Tories" had come out in the open.

By this time, Andrew was hanging around Crawford's military camp regularly. He read all the arms manuals and talked to the soldiers. Though tall and thin, he still had a boyish face, complete with freckles. There was no way he would pass as a soldier. Nevertheless, he was completely fascinated by the events that were taking place before him.

He stayed behind when Major Crawford and his men left camp to join Colonel Abraham Buford's regiment some ten miles to the east.

"Wish I couldda gone with 'em," Andrew told a friend. "I'd show them redcoats a thing or two."

But a day or two later, word came that Buford's troops had been soundly defeated by a British force led by Lieutenant-Colonel Banastre Tarleton. More than one hundred Americans were dead and many more wounded. Soon the wounded patriots were back at Waxhaw Church, Andrew's old schoolhouse.

Now Andrew saw the reality of war for the first time. The straw floor of the church ran red with blood. Wounded soldiers screamed in agony as Elizabeth Jackson and the other women tried to dress their wounds. Some died, and Andrew had to help remove the bodies. It was a horrible scene, especially in a rural farming community that had been quiet and peaceful for so many years.

The sight only made Andrew more bitter toward the British. The redcoats were bringing death and terror to the Carolinas. Soon, it was too dangerous for the settlers to remain in the Waxhaws. There weren't enough soldiers to protect them from the redcoats and the Tory raiders.

Colonel Sumter's troops were camped over the

North Carolina border. The people would be safer there. They took only what they could carry and drove their horses and cattle before them. It was a sad trip. With tears in their eyes, many of the settlers wondered if they would ever see their homes again. For Andrew and the other youngsters, they were leaving the only home they had ever known.

Fortunately, the British force soon moved on and the residents returned to Waxhaw. This time, however, they had Colonel Sumter and six hundred men with them. No one knew how long it would be before the British returned.

Beginning with his brother's death, the events of the war were having a deep effect on Andrew Jackson. He was just four months past his thirteenth birthday, but he was already thinking like a man.

"Robert, we've got to find a way to join the army," he said to his brother.

"They won't take us. We're still too young."

"I might be, but I don't think you are. Maybe I can fool them."

"Too many people know you," Robert said.

No matter. The two brothers went to the nearby army camp and volunteered for duty. Major William Davie accepted both boys. He made Robert a private, but felt Andrew was still too young to be a regular soldier.

Years later, Jackson recalled that he was made "a mounted orderly or messenger, for which I was well fitted, being a good rider and knowing all the roads."

So in mid-July of 1780, Andrew Jackson was made a member of the American army. He was now a Patriot.

Soon after, Major Davie led his company of "dragoons" against the British at a place called Hanging Rock. The Americans won but many Waxhaw fighters were wounded. The Major ordered the two Jackson brothers to lead the wounded home because they knew the way.

They reached the Waxhaws only to learn that the British General Cornwallis had defeated the colonial army under General Gates. When Colonel Sumter fell back to defend the Waxhaws, a British force under Tarleton surprised him and scattered his troops.

Now the Waxhaws was not safe at all. Tarleton's troops were everywhere, looking for lone colonial soldiers. There were also many Tories about now, and Americans had to be suspicious of one another. Upon meeting a stranger on the roads the first question asked was:

"Who are you for?"

And the answer, either "The Congress" or "The King," would tell you if you were facing a friend or an enemy. It was so dangerous that the two Jackson brothers and their mother decided to leave for Charlotte, North Carolina. But things were even worse there. Cornwallis and his troops were not far off. The Jacksons were staying with friends and relatives. All around them armed soldiers were fighting to protect their homes.

In Charlotte, they heard about a local hero named "Nolichucky" Jack Sevier. Sevier lived even further west in the Carolinas than the Waxhaws. He got his nickname from a local river called the Nolichucky. The war hadn't really touched Sevier's area, but he was a man with big ideas and unusual methods. He didn't like the way the British were treating ordinary citizens, so he took action.

Sevier put together his own army of nearly one thousand men. Instead of becoming part of the colonial army, he and his raiders operated on their own. They often dressed and fought like Indians, and they gave the British several solid defeats in the Western District. It was the first good news the people in the region had in a long time.

Inspired by Nolichucky Jack, Andrew and his brother decided to return to the Waxhaws. They were determined to fight for their country. They reached home in January of 1781, and officially joined the militia. This time they were both given muskets and expected to fight like any other soldier. Andrew was not yet fourteen years old.

One night, a short time later, Andrew was on guard duty. Suddenly, the quiet was shattered by a cry that made him jump to his feet.

"It's the Tories. They're here!"

Andrew saw a number of dark figures crouching in the shadows. When they refused to identify themselves he aimed his musket and fired. Gunfire boomed in return. Andrew quickly ducked into the house. He and six others began firing. One of his companions fell dead beside him.

*After Andrew and his brother returned to Waxhaws, they were both given muskets and expected to fight like any other man.*

The smoke from the muskets became so thick it was hard to breathe.

Then Andrew's uncle, James Crawford, was hit. It was beginning to look as if the Tories would storm the house. Andrew Jackson knew that he could easily be killed.

Just then, Andrew and his comrades heard a sound

*A bugle was sounding a cavalry charge. Help had arrived!*

that was music to their ears. A bugle was blaring in the rear of the house. It was sounding a cavalry charge. Help had arrived! Hearing it, the Tories ran for their horses and fled. Upon going outside to meet their rescuers, the Patriots found one of their neighbors, a single man, holding a bugle.

"I didn't have a gun, so I thought it might help to sound a charge," the man said.

The timely notes of the bugle had saved them. A lucky break, indeed. It was Andrew's first real battle, and it easily could have been his last. For the next month, the militia stayed within the Waxhaws, looking for Tories and trying to protect the homes in the area. They sometimes stayed at the homes of neighbors, or at the Waxhaw Church.

On April 9, 1781, their luck ran out. They had gathered at the church under Major Crawford to plan their strategy against the Tories. Without warning, they were set upon by a group of Tories and British soldiers.

Eleven of the forty men in the church were captured immediately. The others fled. Andrew and his brother, Robert, were separated. The Tories burned the Waxhaw Church to the ground.

Andrew and his cousin, Lieutenant Thomas Crawford, tried to cover their tracks by riding through the swampy water of Cain Creek. Andrew used all his skills as a horseman to get across. But his cousin's horse bogged down and he was captured.

Cold and wet, Andrew finally found his brother. The two spent the night at the edge of the swamp, shivering and hungry.

"What'll we do, Andy?" Robert asked. "The men are scattered all over the place. There's Tories everywhere you look."

"I know. Maybe we can make it back to Charlotte and find Ma."

"In the morning we'll try to find some of the others and get outta here," Robert said.

The two brothers huddled together in the dark woods until the sun peeked over the horizon. Slowly and carefully, they made their way toward the Crawford house. They were tired and hungry. Maybe at the Crawfords' they could get some food. They also wanted to tell the family that Thomas had been captured.

But they were only at the house a few minutes when the British burst through the door. A Tory had seen them and informed the redcoats. This time there was no escape. They had been captured.

CHAPTER FOUR

# Prisoner of War

Andrew was frightened. The British soldiers stormed through the house wrecking everything. Within minutes, the British officer ordered the youngster to clean his boots. When Andrew refused, he struck him with his sword. Bruised and bloody, Andrew wondered if the officer was about to kill him. Perhaps he would have done so, had there not been something he wanted.

The soldiers were looking for the house of a patriot named Thompson. One of the Tories had told them that Andrew knew how to get there. So the British soldiers allowed Andrew's wounds to be bandaged enough to stop the bleeding. Then they took him outside and put him on a horse.

"If you value your life, you'll show us to Thompson's house," the officer said. "And no tricks."

Andrew thought quickly. He knew where Thompson lived, all right, yet he didn't want him caught. There was a road that led to the back of Thompson's house. But if he took them that way, Thompson might not see them coming.

"All right, follow me," he said. "I'll show you how to get there."

Instead of taking the back road, Andrew went the long way. He brought the British across an open field, giving Thompson plenty of time to see them coming.

Sure enough, the Patriot spotted the Tories and quickly escaped out the back door. It didn't take Andrew's captors long to figure out what he had done. The youth would have to be punished severely, perhaps even killed.

"This one walks all the way to Camden without food or water," the officer shouted. "No horse, no matter what. In fact, make him run."

Camden was the town where the British prison was located. It was forty miles away. It would have been a very hard walk, even with food and water. Andrew had neither. And he was still weak from the loss of blood caused by his wounds.

Determined to survive, Andrew struggled to keep going. Sometimes he walked. Sometimes they made him run. His wounds ached and throbbed, the blood seeping through the ragged bandages. His head was light, his throat dry and parched. Oh, how he wanted water.

"Can't I have a drink?" he asked, several times.

But the answer was always the same.

"Got my orders, lad. No water."

A few times when they went past a stream, Andrew tried to scoop up just a taste of water, but the British guards wouldn't allow it. They just forced him to run a little harder. There were moments when Andrew didn't think he could continue. But his will was strong. He wanted to find his brother again. And he wouldn't let the British beat him. He was determined to live to fight them again.

"I'll make it," he said to himself. "I've got to."

When they finally reached Camden, Andrew was exhausted. An old jail house served as the British military prison. The old two-story building had a wooden fence constructed around it to make it more secure. That way, the British could crowd more prisoners inside. Andrew was placed in a second-floor room.

A Tory guard came and took Andrew's coat and boots. No one bothered to treat his wounds. Stale bread and a jug of dirty water made up his daily meals. He was in a large room with a number of other prisoners. They had crude, straw bunks, but little else. There was only one window. The men passed the days hoping for their release and talking about fighting the British again.

Andrew asked about his brother several times, but got no answer. He didn't know if Robert was dead or alive. Could he possibly have escaped? Maybe he was a prisoner somewhere in the same building. Why wouldn't they tell him?

Despite the poor treatment and lack of food, Andrew began to feel better as his wounds healed. Within a few days there were new prisoners brought into the room. Then Andrew heard some news that sent shivers up his spine.

"It's the pox," one of the men told him. "It's in the prison here. We're all gonna get it."

*He wondered if he would die alone in this prison.*

"I seen it before," another said. "It can spread like wildfire."

It was true. Smallpox, a deadly disease, had been brought into the prison and was spreading rapidly. Andrew knew how quickly it could kill. He wondered if he would die alone in this prison without knowing how the war would end, or ever seeing his family again. He hated that thought.

But there was hope. In a few days Andrew looked out the window to see American troops camped on a hillside not far away. He had heard stories that General Nathaniel Greene was in the area. Perhaps the Americans would attack and take the prison.

35

Andrew watched the American army every spare moment he could until a carpenter came in and boarded up the window.

"I've got to see what's going on out there," Andrew told the others. He quickly went to work with the only tool he had, a razor that was used to cut up their bread. With it, he managed to cut a two-inch hole from a knot in the wood.

He could see the American soldiers again. It made him feel hopeful, just to see them. Then on the morning of April 25, 1781, Andrew watched as the Americans and British battled close to the prison. At first it looked like the Americans would win. As Andrew remembered many years later:

"Never were hearts more elated than ours at the glitter of American swords, which promised immediate release to us." But . . . "How short was our joy. The roar of our cannon ceased and the sound of our small arms appeared retiring."

The Americans did not manage to get to the prison. By afternoon, they were in retreat, the area overrun by British redcoats. Andrew collapsed in disappointment and anger. Freedom, precious freedom, had seemed so close. And as he lay there, drained of hope, he realized something else. He had the fever. The smallpox was upon him.

If young Andrew might have given up at any time, it was right then and there. Help had been so close; now it was gone, and he was weak with fever. Other prisoners were dying of the disease. The stench inside the prison grew worse. Each day more bodies were carried out. Death was in the air. And in spite of all he had been through, Andrew Jackson was only a boy.

Andrew lost count of the days and months. His fever grew worse. His spirits began to droop. One day he sensed one of the guards in the room, but he didn't stir.

"Andrew Jackson!" the guard barked. "Jackson. Andrew Jackson."

He opened his eyes, but didn't move. What could they possibly want with him now?"

"Get up, Jackson," the guard bellowed. "You're to come with me!"

Slowly, Andrew pulled himself to his feet. The fever made him light-headed and he had to steady himself. The guard was impatient and beckoned Andrew to follow. He was led into the commander's office and what he saw there seemed like a dream.

"Mother! Is it really you?"

Standing before him was Elizabeth Jackson. His beloved mother had come for him. She was smiling, but Andrew could see the lines in her face. They weren't there before the war. It had aged her, all right.

He knew that he didn't look well, either. Then he realized someone else was in the room. It was his brother, Robert. So he had been at the prison after all. But when Andrew took a closer look he could see that his brother was even sicker than he.

Andrew wanted to ask all kinds of questions, but he could see his mother wanted to get them out quickly. Maybe she thought the British would change their minds.

"It was an exchange," she told Andrew, as they walked out the gates of the prison. "I found out you and Robert were here, and when I learned some British prisoners were going to be let go, I asked if you could be released as well."

"I don't know how you did it," Andrew said, weakly. "But I'm sure glad you did."

Elizabeth Jackson had brought a pair of horses. She could see that both her boys had full-blown cases of smallpox. Now, after traveling so far to find them, she wondered if they could survive the journey home.

"You two boys can ride," she said. "I don't mind a little walking."

Andrew could see that Robert had to ride. In fact, he couldn't even mount the horse without help. The younger Jackson looked at his mother and took a deep breath.

"I'm the one who's walking," he said firmly.

The trip home was difficult. Mrs. Jackson gave the boys some bread and smoked meat, and they tried to make Robert as comfortable as possible. But the fever really had a hold on him. He could barely speak. They pressed on, following the trail back to the Waxhaws.

On the second day it rained, a cold, drenching rain. Andrew continued to walk, though he had no coat, hat, or boots. He was getting weaker, but was determined to make it.

By the second night, they were back home in the Waxhaws. Yet Robert was nearly unconscious and Andrew's fever had grown worse from the weather and the endless walking. He was now seriously ill. He didn't even know it when Robert died just two days later.

Now it was Andrew who was fighting for his life. For a while he seemed close to death. Gradually, he began to rally, though for many months afterward he remained weak and tired.

The summer of 1781 passed slowly. Life was not the same in the Waxhaws. Many friends and neighbors were now dead. Food was scarce, farms ruined. The only good news was that the war to the north was going well. The British had finally been driven from the Carolinas.

Andrew made a slow, steady recovery. He was moving about more, beginning to do small chores around the house. Once she was certain that her only remaining son was all right, Mrs. Jackson told Andrew she had to go away.

"It's your cousins, Joseph and William," she said. "We've learned they're on a prison ship in Charles Town Harbor. I must go to try to help them. Two others are going with me, but we must leave now."

The news upset Andrew. He knew his mother would want to help the Crawford boys. She had helped raise both of them. He insisted that he should go along with her. But his mother knew Andrew wasn't strong enough yet. She told him to stay behind.

"Mother, what will I do?" he asked with dismay.

It wasn't like the old days. His uncle, James, was still away at the war. His brothers were dead. Several of his cousins were prisoners, others were in the army, or perhaps dead. No one really knew. And now, just a short time after his return home, his mother wanted to leave him.

"You'll be fine," she said. "You're getting stronger every day and you know how to take care of things around here."

While Andrew knew she was right, it didn't help to ease the pain. His mother was going on a dangerous trip. The war for America's independence was still being fought, and there was much disease on the prison ships. His cousins were already sick. He couldn't help feeling worried and frightened.

Although Elizabeth Jackson told her son that she would return, she knew there was a chance she would not. Her last words to her only surviving son were words of advice, a code for him to live by.

She told Andrew he would need friends in life, and that he would make them by being honest, and keep them by being steadfast. She also said he should fight for the things he believed in, and settle his fights fairly.

"Never tell a lie, Andrew," she finished, "nor take what is not yours. If you have a personal dispute, or are slandered, settle it yourself."

Andrew thought about her words as she rode off, and vowed to remember them all his life. He stood in the doorway of their old home and watched his mother vanish into the distance. Mrs. Jackson had set her personal feelings and safety aside to do her duty. That quality, too, was something Andrew would always remember.

Andrew grew stronger as he waited for news. There was not much to do around home. He tried to make some minor repairs in the house, but there were no crops, no planting, and no reason to plant. He didn't know what the future would bring.

In October of 1781, American forces defeated Lord Cornwallis at Yorktown. In effect, that battle was the end of the war. Though the peace treaty wouldn't be signed until September of 1783, there was little fighting after Yorktown. The Patriots had won! America was free!

It should have been a great moment for Andrew. But he could not celebrate, not without news of his mother. When he finally got the word a month later, it nearly destroyed him.

His mother had found his cousins. But both were very sick. Joseph Crawford couldn't be helped and soon died. Elizabeth Jackson worked hard and long to nurse William back to health. In doing so, she came down with the fever herself.

On a cold November day in 1781, Elizabeth Jackson died. Like other victims of smallpox, she was buried in an unmarked grave near Charles Town Harbor.

This latest tragedy was a terrible blow to a youngster not yet fifteen years old. With the news of her death, he received a small package containing the clothes his mother had taken with her. That was all that remained.

His relatives tried to talk to him. But the sobbing Andrew just wanted to be by himself. He now had only the memories of Hugh, Robert, and his beloved mother, Elizabeth.

"I felt utterly alone," he recalled in later years, "and just tried to recall her last words to me."

# A Surprise Inheritance

P rospects for the future were not bright. To many in the Waxhaws, as in other regions throughout the young land, victory seemed rather hollow. Andrew looked around at his own family and friends. Loved ones were dead. Many of the homes in the area had been damaged or destroyed by the British and the Tories. Many needed repairs, but there was no one around to make them.

Fields that had once held crops were now overgrown with weeds. There hadn't been a good crop planted in several years. On many farms, there wouldn't be one planted ever again. The Waxhaw Church was in ruins.

Andrew watched as his friends and relatives tried to pick up the pieces of their lives. He helped wherever he could, repairing roofs, rebuilding corrals, tilling the land. America had won its independence, but the war had left Andrew Jackson an orphan, living first with one relative, then another. He always worked hard to earn his keep, but his heart was not in his work. He tried school again, but it didn't last long, either. He was just too restless.

*Many homes were damaged or destroyed.*

He thought constantly about his mother and brothers. *If only they had survived, things would be different,* he thought over and over again. He even thought about his father, and about the stories his mother told him of coming to the Waxhaws from Ireland to start a new life.

*We should all be together now,* he said, to himself, *working hard and building a future.*

Andrew felt bitter when he thought about his family. He missed his mother and brothers terribly. His relatives could see the deep sadness he carried within him. They didn't know how to help him. He spent more time racing with his horse. He began to bet on other races. But nothing he did seemed to inspire him.

His relatives began to wonder just what would become of Andrew. He was wild and undisciplined. Perhaps one day, they thought, he would just disappear into the frontier, never to be seen again. In the meantime he continued to gamble and spend time with a rough crowd.

This went on until March of 1883, when Andrew was barely sixteen. Then one morning he received a letter from Ireland. He wondered what news it could possibly contain. He still had family in Carrickfergus, but he hadn't heard from them for a long, long time. When he opened the letter, the first thing that struck him was more bad news.

"It's my grandfather, Hugh Jackson," he said, as his relatives gathered around. "He's dead."

Andrew didn't remember his grandfather, who was a merchant in Carrickfergus, but his Uncle Robert and several others did. They told Andrew he had been a good and honorable man. But what did the rest of the letter say, they asked?

"I can't believe this," Andrew said, continuing to stare at the letter. "Maybe my luck is changing."

Those around him craned their necks to see the letter. What in the world could he be talking about?

"Andrew, what is it? Tell us."

"Grandfather had an estate valued at about three hundred pounds, and he's left it to my family . . . to me."

Three hundred pounds was well over a thousand dollars in American money. In those days it was a lot of money, especially for a sixteen-year-old boy. Since he was the only Jackson left in America, the money was all his. It was hard for Andrew to believe.

"It's an inheritance, Andrew," one of his relatives said. "You'll have to decide what you want to do with it."

The first thing he had to do was get the money. To

do that, he'd have to travel to Charleston (the city's name had been changed from Charles Town after the war). Andrew liked that idea. He had always vowed to return to the big city. So much had happened since he first saw the city, Andrew thought. For the first time since the war, he felt excited and hopeful.

As soon as he could gather his belongings and pack them on his horse, Andrew left for Charleston. During the journey he wondered what he would do with all the money his grandfather had left him. For the first time in his life, he had options.

He could go back and put the old farm in shape. Or he could even go to college or law school. Then again, perhaps he could just put up a fine cabin somewhere and live by himself. He sure knew how to take care of himself by now.

Andrew laughed aloud. It was funny how quickly money changed things. One day, he was a boy with no place to go and very little to do. Now, there was so much he could do that he didn't know which way to turn.

When he reached Charleston, he quickly stabled his horse and got a room at a fancy hotel called the Quarter House Tavern. He washed up and changed his clothes. Then he sought out the lawyer who had sent him the letter. Within an hour, the paperwork had been completed. Young Andrew Jackson now had more money in his pocket than he had ever dreamed of having.

What should he do? He went to a tailor and was measured for several fine, new suits. Then he took a walk through town, where he found himself haunted by memories of the cattle drive, the war, and his family. By the time he returned to the Quarter House Tavern, he was exhausted. In no time, he was sound asleep.

The next day Andrew felt rested and refreshed. He looked at the pile of silver money once again. His future was definitely brighter. And, being a young man who had seen very difficult times, he decided to stay in Charleston and have some fun.

He met a group of young people and began to drift with them. Much of their time was spent at the Charleston race track. Andrew loved betting on the horses and this was the first time he had seen a real track. The track itself was set off with wooden rails, and the spectators gathered around the outside. The men smoked cigars and sipped strong whiskey as they exchanged money and cheered for their favorite horses.

Andrew bet heavily. He lost money, but enjoyed every minute of it. His life had no plan. One day melted into the next. Whenever someone asked Andrew about his future, or what he was going to do with his life, he would push the question aside.

"How do I know?" he would say. "Why do I have to decide anything now? I'm having too much fun to worry about the future."

As for the inheritance, Andrew acted as though it would last forever. He did not keep count of how much he was spending.

One night when Andrew returned to his hotel, the clerk reminded him that his bill hadn't been paid in three weeks. He also owed money to the tailor and the hat maker.

Back in his room, the written bill was waiting for him. It totaled about forty pounds. He started looking around for money to see how much he had left. Before he knew it, he was tearing the room apart, searching through the bureau drawers, and even under the bed. There was nothing. Not a pound. He turned his pockets out. Same result.

"It's gone," he said, almost in disbelief. "The money's all gone. I've got nothing left."

He shook his head, then looked again. Sure enough, Andrew had spent or lost all of his grandfather's money. He couldn't even pay for his room. Still upset, he went down to the stable. Maybe if he rode his horse out into the countryside, his head would clear. Then he'd know what to do.

When he reached the stable he spotted a group of men throwing dice. They were gambling and there was a great deal of money passing back and forth. Andrew got his horse from the stable and walked past the men.

"That's a fine looking animal you've got there," one of the men shouted. "If you're a gamblin' man, you'll take my wager against your horse. How much?"

*A gamblin' man!* That was the reason Andrew was broke. He had gambled his inheritance away. Now this man was asking him to gamble the last thing he owned, his horse. He thought about the money he owed. He looked at the horse once again, then the man.

"Forty pounds," he answered.

"You got yourself a bet, sport," the man said, handing Andrew a pair of dice. "You roll 'em."

Andrew knelt down within the circle of men. He could feel the tension building up as he shook the dice. Holding his breath, he rolled them.

"You won," one of men shouted at him. Another slapped him on the back. "Good throw, boy. You did it."

The other man handed Andrew the forty pounds, shaking his head as he did.

"This was your lucky day," he said. "But I still like your horse. Anytime you want to try again, I'll be here."

But, for Andrew, there would be no next time. He looked closely at the big bay horse with the black markings on its lower legs and tail. He had helped raise it from a young colt. His Uncle Robert had given it to him for his very own. It was bad enough that he had gambled away his inheritance. But to wager his horse?

"What kind of person have you become, Andrew Jackson?" he asked himself. He answered his own question. "A person I don't like very much."

Andrew hugged his horse several times. Then he went back to the hotel and paid his bill. He also paid the tailor and hat maker. After that, he packed quickly and rode out of Charleston the same way he had entered . . . without a cent in his pockets.

# CHAPTER SIX

# The Wanderer

Andrew rode slowly back toward the Waxhaws. He wondered how his relatives would feel about him now that he'd lost his money. He still wasn't sure what he was going to do, but he knew he couldn't live the way he had in Charleston. As he himself put it in later years, he headed home to the Waxhaws with "new spirits infused into me."

His aunts and uncles weren't too pleased when they heard what had happened. Though he said he had learned his lesson, they had no way of knowing whether he was telling the truth. In addition, he seemed as restless as ever. He still wasn't sure what he wanted to do with his life. As much as he loved his relatives, there was really nothing to keep him in the Waxhaws any longer.

One cold December day in 1784, seventeen-year-old Andrew Jackson rode away from the only home he had ever known. Although he didn't know it at the time, he would never return.

Without any real plan, he drifted to Salisbury, North Carolina. Salisbury was not nearly as large as Charleston, but it had two main streets that crossed at the town square. There was a public well there, and people gathered for water and conversation all day long. Several

*One cold December day, Andrew Jackson rode away from the only home he had ever known.*

shops and stores surrounded the square. Beyond that there were small houses and cabins, most of which had nice lawns and gardens.

Andrew spent Christmas in Salisbury at an inn called the Rowan House. There he met a lawyer named Spruce Macay, a middle-aged man respected by the townspeople. Andrew persuaded Macay to take him on as a law student. Finally, he had made a concrete decision. He would stay in Salisbury at the Rowan House and study law.

So the youngster from the Waxhaws joined two other young men in Mr. Macay's office and began his studies. In those days, especially on the frontier, students did not have to attend a college or law school. They could assist a certified lawyer and, when they were ready, take an exam given by a judge.

Andrew tackled his studies hard, but he also had fun. He continued to attend horse races and cock fights, where two roosters fought to the death, and the men placed bets on which rooster would win. He played a lot of cards and went to socials where he danced with the young ladies of the town.

Just a few months from his eighteenth birthday, Andrew was a tall boy, thin, with a long face, still scarred from the smallpox. He continued to carry the scar from the British sword which ran up his forehead and disappeared into his thick head of hair. He may not have been called handsome, but the ladies would certainly stop to watch him pass.

A young lady named Nancy Jarret, a relative of Spruce Macay, saw Andrew quite often in those days. Her memories of him were quite strong.

"His ways and manners were quite captivating," she recalled later. "We all knew that he was wild, that he was gambling some. . . . When he was calm he talked slowly and with good selected language. But . . . animated . . .

51

*He attended cock fights, where two roosters were trained to fight to the death.*

he would talk fast with a very marked North-Irish brogue. Either calm or animated, there was something about him I cannot describe except to say that it was a presence."

He still had a wild streak in him, and he still liked to gamble occasionally. Yet he also had a quality that would later draw people to him, and sometimes overpower them. Andrew Jackson impressed people. Once they met him, they remembered him. Nancy Jarret called it a presence. Whatever it was, it was a powerful force and a major part of his charm. In later years, even his enemies would give in to it.

For two years, Andrew studied law with Spruce Macay. Then he went to work for Colonel John Stokes, another Salisbury lawyer. Stokes was considered one of the most brilliant lawyers in North Carolina. He was also a war hero. He had lost a hand in battle and wore a silver knob in its place. Andrew enjoyed studying with him. Finally, on September 26, 1787, Andrew was given an examination by Judges Samuel Ashe and John F. Williams.

Among other things, the two judges concluded that, "Andrew Jackson was a person of unblemished moral character" and was "competent in his knowledge of the law." Andrew Jackson was now a lawyer, with a certificate to practice in the courts. The restless boy from the frontier was finally on the way to making something of his life. He was a lawyer.

When Andrew Jackson went to court he was a sight to see. He was twenty years old, a full six feet tall, still slender and straight as an arrow. He wore a brown broadcloth coat and ruffled shirt. His thick, dark red hair was carefully combed back from his high forehead. He moved easily and with a certain kind of grace. Nancy Jarret wrote:

"His eyes were handsome, a kind of steel-blue. I have talked with him a great many times and never saw him avert his eyes from me for an instant."

Shortly after he received his law certificate, it was suggested he go out on the road. In those days, lawyers and judges often traveled to different towns together, hearing the cases that had built up since their last visit.

One of the judges told Andrew he should go "up West," In this case, up West was the Western District of North Carolina, just beyond the Allegheny Mountains.

"They need lawyers up there," the judge said. "It will be a good place for a young man like you to get experience and establish a reputation."

Andrew did not go right away. Instead, he rode around the Salisbury area and didn't make much money. In fact, he even worked in a store for awhile. Then one day a lawyer friend of his, John McNairy, came looking for him. McNairy had a definite plan.

"I've been named a judge by the governor of North Carolina for the Western District," McNairy said. "And as a judge, I can appoint a public prosecutor. Want the job?"

"You bet I do," Andrew said, without hesitation. "When do we leave?"

"As soon as we can."

It was April of 1788 when the two friends set out for the settlement at French Lick, some five hundred miles to the west. It was a dangerous journey. They would be heading over the mountains to places where few people had been before. Many of the trails were not mapped. Others were almost impossible to travel on. Andrew and John would have to provide their own food by hunting, and always would have to be on the lookout for hostile Indians.

Each of them brought two horses for the journey, one to ride, and the other to carry their packs. The pack horses carried law books, extra clothing, and as much food (mostly smoked meat and biscuits) as they could safely take. Andrew also had two pistols slung from his saddle, and a rifle at the ready, lashed to the top of his pack. Let the dangers come. As always, Andrew Jackson was willing to face them.

The journey did not turn out quite as expected. By the late summer of 1788, the two arrived at Jonesborough, in the Western District. They were still several hundred miles from French Lick. At Jonesborough, there were about fifty cabins set up in the town, along with a log courthouse. There was also a great deal of legal work, mostly cases involving land boundaries and unpaid debts. The two friends decided to stay.

"There's a wagon train heading for French Lick this fall," Andrew told McNairy. "Maybe we can get away by then."

The two men found a cabin in which to live and went to work. They solved many of the legal problems of the settlement in a simple and honest way. The townspeople grew to like both of them.

When they weren't working as judge and prosecutor, the two pitched in building log cabins and clearing land. Andrew even found time to get involved in one high-stakes horse race in which his horse lost. He had been bragging about his horse and bet heavily on him.

"Maybe someday I'll learn my lesson," he told himself. "But I haven't learned it yet."

In the fall it was time to move on. About forty families came to Jonesborough on the way to French Lick, which had been renamed Nashville. They had been promised government land there as payment for their service during the war. They would be the first group to travel across the newly opened Cumberland Road, a rugged trail across the Cumberland mountains some one hundred and eighty miles through Cherokee Indian country.

It was a difficult journey. The trail was so rough in spots that not all the wagons made it. Food was hard to find and the men couldn't always hunt for fear of Indians. One night, in fact, when Andrew was on guard duty, he realized the camp was surrounded by Indians.

Without making a sound, he woke the men. Knowing the Indians wouldn't attack until morning, the settlers had a chance to circle the wagons and put up barriers. When the Indians saw they had lost the element of surprise, they gave up the attack.

On October 26, the wagons came to the crest of a hill overlooking the Cumberland River. Andrew and John McNairy looked at each other.

"That's Nashville?" McNairy said.

"I guess so," said Andrew with a grin.

What they saw looked nothing like Charleston. It didn't even look like Jonesborough. Part of the settlement was built inside a ragged, uneven fence, put there to keep grazing buffalo out of the city. Inside the fence were two taverns, two stores, a distillery (for making whiskey), the courthouse, a group of simple log cabins, bare tents, and wagon camps. There were also a number of farms and cabins scattered about the countryside within ten miles or so of the city. It was an ordinary frontier city.

The courthouse, built from rough-cut logs, was just eighteen feet square with a porch on one side. Inside, it was a filthy mess, with benches strewn about, and doors hanging from their hinges. It was obvious that not much law had been practiced there. But within a week, Andrew and John had the place cleaned up. On November 3, John McNairy took the judge's bench at age twenty-six. And his prosecutor was the twenty-one-year-old Andrew Jackson.

In town, there were many debtors, people who owed a great deal of money. But they had joined together as a group, and refused to pay whenever someone tried to collect. There was also always the threat of violence.

The new prosecutor, however, proved to be a strong man and was on the side of the debt collectors. Within a month, Andrew had gotten about seventy debts paid back, whether it was with money, land, traded goods, or work.

The landowners took an immediate liking to this young, tough lawyer. They hired him for other jobs. Because cash was scarce, when it came time to pay him it was often the same story:

"Would you take a piece of land as payment?" they would ask.

"Why not?" Andrew would say, and before long he was a landowner himself.

He had chosen to stay at the home of the widow Donelson instead of at one of the inns in the town. This decision would change his life forever.

# CHAPTER SEVEN

# Lawyer, Landowner, Husband

Shortly after arriving in Nashville, Andrew met a young lawyer named John Overton. Overton had come from Kentucky to Nashville to practice law on the frontier. He welcomed the judge and prosecutor to Nashville with enthusiasm, then suggested they board at the home of Mrs. John Donelson.

John McNairy decided to stay in town, but Andrew took Overton up on his offer. The two men would share a cabin outside the main house, but would help with household chores and take their meals at the Donelson table. It worked well for everyone. The Donelsons were the largest family in Nashville, and one of the most powerful. They welcomed a young man like Andrew Jackson, if for no other reason than to protect them from Indians.

John Donelson and his wife were from Virginia. They had been rich landowners before losing much of their money in a bad business deal. After losing his money

*In Nashville, Andrew shared a cabin with John Overton.*

in 1778, Mr. Donelson and a man named James Robertson decided to start a town in the Cumberland Valley.

Robertson traveled by land. John Donelson, his wife, eleven children, other relatives, friends and neighbors, journeyed to the Cumberland by river in a small fleet of flatboats. The boats started out in December of 1779. After an adventurous voyage, full of tricky river currents, hostile Indians, and smallpox, they came to the end of

59

the two-thousand-mile journey on April 24, 1780. That same day, young Andrew Jackson was peering through a knothole at Camden Prison, watching the British fend off an American attack.

John Donelson stayed in the Cumberland until, several years later, a flood and an Indian treaty caused him to lose his land. He then moved the family to Kentucky and settled there. But a short time later, John Donelson was mysteriously killed. Most felt he had been unlucky enough to run into hostile Indians. But the family claimed it was white outlaws.

Shortly after her husband's death, Mrs. Donelson returned to the Cumberland Valley, where several of her married children had stayed. She set up a house there, and before long John Overton, and then Andrew Jackson, were boarding with her. There, Andrew met Mrs. Donelson's youngest and most beautiful daughter, Rachel. She had come home from Kentucky just a few weeks before Andrew's arrival.

It was John Overton who first told Andrew Rachel's sad story. It seemed that Rachel Donelson had married a man named Lewis Robards in Kentucky in 1785. Rachel was not yet eighteen when she married Robards. The marriage wasn't a good one from the start.

Overton told Andrew that Robards was wildly jealous of any man who even looked at Rachel. And in those days, many did. One of her relatives later remembered young Rachel as a woman of "medium height, beautifully molded form, and full red lips." Her glowing face was always "rippling with smiles and dimples. She was irresistible."

Rachel and Lewis Robards lived at his mother's home in Virginia for about three years. John Overton was also living there at the time. The real trouble began when a young law student named Peyton Short began boarding there. Robards became so jealous of the attention shown Rachel by Short that he finally ordered his wife from the house.

So Rachel traveled to her mother's home in Nashville, and there she met Andrew Jackson. Though Andrew felt he could not pursue a married woman, there was definitely an immediate attraction between the two. As one boy who worked at the Donelson home observed:

"Mr. Jackson was always polite, and he was particularly so to the beautiful Mrs. Robards."

Yet at that time Andrew was too busy with his law practice to see much of Rachel Robards. Early in 1789 the court's season in Nashville ended. It was time for Andrew and John McNairy to go out on the road once again.

The area they needed to cover was a strip of land fifty miles long and twenty miles wide in the Cumberland Valley. The judge and prosecutor stopped at all the tiny settlements along the way to settle arguments and claims. They also dealt with any lawbreakers being held for trial in local jails. It could be a long wait for a trial in some cases, since judges only had to hold court in a settlement twice a year.

It was a time of contrasts in the young American

nation. As men like Andrew Jackson and John McNairy began their trip in the spring of 1789, important events were taking place back East in Philadelphia. The Constitution of the United States had been approved, setting up the basic government that we know today. And in April, George Washington was sworn in as the country's first president.

Yet on the frontier, not a day passed when the settlers' lives weren't in danger. Everyone had to keep a gun at his ready. Hostile Indians might be anywhere.

During those days in Nashville, many people were killed, including women and children, and countless others were wounded. In fact, someone was killed an average of once every ten days around Nashville for the entire year of 1789.

Andrew Jackson's life was considerably more exciting than that of the average lawyer today. In March of that year he saved three friends from drowning in a flooded river. Then in June he heard that James Robertson, who had founded Nashville with John Donelson, had been wounded by Indians at Robertson's Station. Andrew was traveling nearby and raced to the Station.

"What happened?" he asked.

"Injun attacks. They wounded Mr. Robertson," a man said. "They headed upriver."

"Let's get some men and get after them," Andrew said.

"That's jest what we're doin'," the man said.

Before long, Andrew joined eighteen other men and tracked the Indians some ten miles. The party of settlers attacked at dawn. When the gunfire had died down, several Indians lay dead and the others had fled. It was a big victory for the settlers of the Cumberland, and Andrew Jackson was right in the middle of it.

Besides being a straight and honest lawyer, Andrew was becoming known as a man who could be counted on in a dangerous situation. He was a good friend to have.

He would go to any lengths to help a client, including making long, and sometimes dangerous, journeys. Several times, he traveled the two hundred miles from Nashville back to Jonesborough on legal business. Once, he rode more than five hundred miles downriver to Natchez, Mississippi, where he met Thomas Green, a former Kentuckian. Mr. Green had a brother in Nashville, and Andrew went to Natchez to help the two brothers with some legal problems. They, too, liked the young lawyer very much.

"We will always welcome you in Natchez, my friend," Thomas Green said.

"That's good to know," said Andrew. "Perhaps I will return someday."

During these trips he was alone, his two horses his only companions. He rode on rough-cut trails. It was tiring to travel and he always had to be on the lookout for wild animals or unfriendly Indians.

If he was lucky enough to come upon a cabin or a small settlement along the road, he would get a hot meal and some supplies. But many a night he was not so lucky. He didn't even dare build a fire for fear the Indians would see it.

In between his travels, he would return to Nashville, if only for a short time. And each time, he would hear of the continuing troubles between Rachel and Lewis Robards. In fact, Robards had come to Nashville to try to get his wife back.

While he was in Nashville, Robards grew jealous of Andrew. He claimed the young lawyer and Rachel had a fondness for each other. Though drawn to Rachel, Andrew Jackson would never pursue another man's wife.

"You do your wife a grave injustice," he told Robards. "Not only are the things you are saying untrue, but you have not treated Rachel as a lady."

Robards didn't like what he heard. He challenged Andrew to a fistfight, but the lawyer had another suggestion.

"If you want satisfaction, a simple fistfight will not do," he said, firmly. "Meet me as a gentleman would with dueling pistols."

Robards turned down the offer to duel. But the two men were on a collision course. Andrew's strong dislike for Lewis Robards slowly drew him deeper into the life of Rachel Donelson Robards. In June of 1790, Robards returned to Kentucky on business. A short time later, Rachel followed, perhaps to give the marriage one last chance.

It did not work. The couple began quarreling almost immediately, and this time Rachel became frightened. She sent word back to Nashville that she was afraid for her safety. She had to get away from her husband.

Robards then made the following events part of the

official record of the Court of Quarter Sessions in Harrodsburgh, Kentucky. The record shows that "Rachel Robards did, on the day of July, 1790, elope from her husband . . . with another man."

That man was Andrew Jackson.

The language of the court made it sound as if she ran off with Andrew. But he was simply following instructions from the Donelson family to fetch her. He went to Kentucky to bring the unhappy Rachel home. He accompanied her to the home of her sister, Jane, the wife of Colonel Robert Hayes. He left her there and went back to work.

Robards returned in August to try to save his marriage. He failed. And when Andrew came back from a journey in early 1791, he found Mrs. Donelson and Rachel very upset.

"Lewis is threatening to divorce my daughter," Mrs. Donelson said.

"That can't be," Andrew exclaimed. "It's impossible."

Divorce was very rare on the frontier back then. It just didn't happen. And when it did, the woman was always looked down on. Despite the problems and despite his own feelings, Andrew felt the Robards should stay married.

But when Rachel said she feared for her safety and maybe even her life, Andrew could keep his personal feelings out of the matter no longer.

"Nothing will happen to you," he said firmly. "I can

promise you that much. Lewis Robards will never get a chance to harm you."

His strong words were a comfort. But Rachel wanted to be far away from Robards. She learned that a Colonel John Stark was taking a party of travelers down the Mississippi by flatboat to Natchez. That's where she wanted to go, especially when she learned that Andrew knew the Green family there.

Colonel Stark agreed to take her, but he had one request.

"I'm not a young man anymore," he said. "There's always a chance we'll run into Indians and I'd feel better if there were an extra man aboard to look after the lady."

John Overton couldn't go. Neither could any of Rachel's brothers or brothers-in-law. Because of the situation with Robards, they hesitated to ask Andrew, but he was the only one left.

"I'll go," Andrew said immediately. "How can I say no? The Donelsons have all been so good to me."

Colonel Stark's flatboat left Nashville early in 1791, drifting north on the Cumberland to the Ohio River, then down to the Mississippi and southward. The voyage wasn't difficult, but both Andrew and Rachel must have wondered what life in Natchez would bring.

Rachel was welcomed by the Greens and made to feel at home immediately. As much as he hated to leave, Andrew wasted no time mounting a horse and heading back to Nashville. Rachel was safe, and he had business waiting. He made the three-hundred-mile journey as quickly as he could. Once he was back in Nashville, though, events took a drastic turn.

Instead of looking for Rachel again, Lewis Robards asked the Virginia General Assembly for permission to divorce her (in those days, a divorce could only be granted by a legislative act). It was John Overton who first heard the news. He told Andrew immediately.

"Divorce. You mean Rachel is free of him?" Andrew said.

"Quite free," Overton said. "I heard it from Robards' mother herself. Mrs. Donelson wants one of her boys to go back to Natchez and tell Rachel so she can come home."

That was all Andrew Jackson had to hear. At long last, he no longer had to hide his feelings about Rachel. She was no longer a married woman.

He went to Mrs. Donelson and announced that he was the one to go to Natchez. Then he asked Mrs. Donelson for "permission to offer my hand and heart to your daughter."

Mrs. Donelson couldn't believe her ears. She answered quickly.

"Mr. Jackson, would you sacrifice your life to save my poor child's good name?"

"Ten thousand lives if I had them," said Andrew.

Within hours, he was rushing back to Natchez, pushing his horses to the limit. This time he was going to see the woman he loved. He could admit that now. When at last he reached Natchez and broke the news of the divorce to Rachel she was crushed.

*Andrew Jackson and Rachel Donelson Robards were married in
August 1791.*

"I expected him to kill me, but this is worse," she
said, quietly.

All Rachel could think of was the shame that went
with divorce. But Andrew talked to her, sternly and tenderly at the same time.

"You cannot allow this man to ruin your life," he
told her. "You are still a beautiful young woman and
there is another man who would like your hand in
marriage."

Suddenly, Rachel realized what Andrew was saying.

She looked into his blue eyes and knew how much he loved her. Then Andrew answered her final question.

"I've spoken to your mother and she gives us her blessing," he said.

On a warm August afternoon in 1791, Andrew Jackson and Rachel Donelson Robards stood hand in hand in the elegant parlor of the Green home in Natchez. With candles flickering in the crystal chandelier and the silk curtains drawn back to let even more light in, Andrew and Rachel exchanged marriage vows. They were both twenty-four years old.

They even had a place to live. The Greens had given Andrew a small log house overlooking the Mississippi River at a place called Bayou Pierre. The house was payment for Andrew's legal services.

That night, the newlyweds looked out over the mighty river and then into each other's eyes. It was a miracle that they had found each other.

# CHAPTER EIGHT

# A Busy Life

The bride and groom spent a beautiful summer at Bayou Pierre. The days were warm and sunny. They entertained a constant stream of newfound friends. Life in Natchez was relaxing and carefree. Andrew knew it couldn't go on forever, but Rachel hoped it could.

"We must return to Nashville soon," Andrew said, on a bright September day. "I have business piling up and there are more people than ever coming to the valley. It's going to be a busy time there."

Rachel looked at him with sad eyes. "I suppose you must," she said. "But I have never been as happy as I've been here with you."

"I know," he said.

In October of 1791, the Jacksons returned to Nashville. At first, it was a happy homecoming. The large Donelson family and all of Andrew's friends gathered to welcome the newlyweds back. There were parties and celebrations, feasts of beef and corn, homegrown potatoes and fresh-baked bread. After dinner, a fiddler and a caller were brought in, and everyone would square dance, hootin' and hollerin' far into the night.

It didn't take the newlyweds long to find a place to

live. Rachel's brother, John, was selling Poplar Grove, his small farm on the south side of the Cumberland River. There was a cozy little log house, with the land around the house cleared. Rachel could have the gardens she loved so much. She took to fixing up the house and Andrew went back to work.

With new settlers pouring into the Cumberland Valley the legal work was mounting up. Many had bought land they'd never seen while back East. When they arrived to claim the land, they found that they had been swindled; the land wasn't really there. It had been sold to them illegally. Sometimes it was Indian land that could not be sold.

Andrew Jackson was now a very busy lawyer. Because he spent so many hours in court and on the trail, Rachel seldom saw him. He seemed to spend all his time traveling to Jonesborough and back, a long two-hundred-mile journey. And each time he left, Rachel would worry until she saw him safely at her door once again.

When she asked why he had to travel so much, Andrew said the reason was simple. He wanted to make more money. The sooner he did that, he said, the sooner he could spend more time with her.

Andrew continued working very hard for the next two years. From time to time there would be trouble with the Cherokee Indians and the men would have to fight. Andrew had one or two close calls, but rarely let danger stop him. It was part of frontier life.

By December of 1793, the Indian problems had quieted down enough for Andrew and John Overton to plan a trip to Jonesborough. While they were there, Overton heard some shocking news.

"You won't believe this, Andrew," he said. "But Lewis Robards never divorced Rachel. He's petitioning for divorce now."

"What!" Andrew exclaimed. "That's impossible. He divorced her once already. He can't do it a second time."

"Not according to this," Overton said, holding up a piece of paper. "The Virginia legislature only gave him permission to sue for divorce in Kentucky. He had two years in which to do it. He never did. So now he's finally going ahead with it."

Much to Andrew's dismay Overton's information was correct. When they had heard that Robards divorced Rachel two years earlier, it had been strictly on the word of others. No one had seen the papers. Overton suggested that Andrew and Rachel marry for a second time. At first, Andrew wouldn't hear of it.

"Everyone knows we're married. We've been married for two years," Andrew said. "To marry again would be admitting the first one wasn't legal."

But after finding that Robards had not divorced Rachel in 1791, but in fact in 1793, Andrew changed his mind. He spoke to Rachel.

"I think we should marry again so there are no problems later," he told his wife. "Everyone who matters knows we've been married for two years."

So in January of 1794, Andrew and Rachel were married for a second time in a simple ceremony at Nashville. There was no celebrating this time. And the need for a second ceremony seemed to take some of the happiness out of Rachel Jackson forever.

In later years, when Andrew had political enemies, the whole question would come back to haunt Rachel once more. Yet anyone questioning Rachel's good name had better not do so from close range. As one historian said:

"Andrew Jackson's pistols were in order, and for thirty-three years they kept slanderers at bay."

Hoping that the Robards business was behind them, Andrew returned to his work. With so many new settlers in the region, his personal fortune was piling up. He was also beginning to realize that all the years of being paid in land had made him a very big landowner.

He decided to try to turn some of the land into profit. Hoping to open a general store, he traveled to Philadelphia in 1795 to sell nearly one hundred thousand acres of land. In return, he wanted to buy goods to stock the store.

Andrew made a deal, selling his land. But he didn't get cash. Instead, he received a series of notes, payable at the rate of one a year. So when he went to buy the goods, he used the notes. But he was responsible for paying for the notes if the man who issued them couldn't pay. It was not a pleasant experience. Even though he was a lawyer, Andrew was unused to big city business dealings. Being from the frontier, he would have to learn the hard way.

When he returned to the Cumberland after three months, big news waited for him. The Western District where he lived had a good chance to become a full-fledged state. There were already more than the sixty thousand settlers needed to qualify for statehood. A convention was called in January of 1796 to write a state constitution. Andrew Jackson was elected to be one of the delegates. He was still several months away from his twenty-ninth birthday, and while he may not have realized it then, his political career had begun.

The constitutional convention lasted nearly a month. When it ended on February 7, the delegates gave the federal government forty-nine days to decide on statehood. Part of the proposed constitution allowed residents to vote after living in the state for just six months. It also gave boats free use of the Mississippi River.

The delegates chose the name "Tennessee" for their new state. Many say Andrew Jackson proposed the name. The Tennessee was a river that cut through the center of the territory (the origin of the word "Tennessee" is unknown).

While waiting to hear about statehood, Andrew ran into problems with his store. The man who had issued the notes in exchange for land couldn't make the payment. Andrew was told that he had better make good in cold cash.

The profits from the store would not pay for the notes, either. So Andrew traded the store to a man named Elijah Robertson for thirty-three thousand acres of land, which he sold for twenty-five cents an acre to help pay the debt. He was learning how to be a shrewd business-

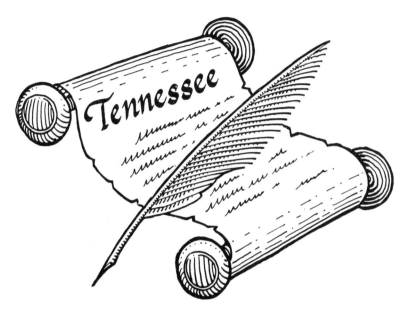

*In June of 1796, Tennessee became a state.*

man, a skill he would need often during the course of his life.

Then in June of 1796, Tennessee became a state. The old Indian fighter, "Nolichucky Jack," John Sevier, became its first governor. Andrew Jackson was elected its first representative to the Congress of the United States.

Before leaving to take his seat in Congress that fall, Andrew bought another piece of land. This one covered six hundred and forty acres near Poplar Grove. The land was known as Hunter's Hill and sat high above the Cumberland River. On it he built a large frame house, still a rare sight in rural Tennessee. While most of the homes in the area were still built from logs, Andrew's two-story home was framed from timber cut into beams and planks. It was the largest house in the Nashville area.

"I want you to have everything you want, the finest things," Andrew told his wife. "You make up the list and I'll send to Philadelphia for them."

Rachel enjoyed every minute of planning for the new house. She ordered tables and chairs, mirrors and chandeliers, and even a harpsichord, so there could be music in their new home. Rachel was overjoyed, but for one thing. She would have everything she wanted . . . except the company of her husband. Andrew was leaving for Washington in November.

"I don't think Congress will be for me," he told her before he left. "I can't see myself just settin', talkin', and votin'. I'd rather be out there doing something."

"Then why go, Mr. Jackson?" Rachel asked.

"Because the people have elected me."

"Then I suppose you must go."

Andrew nodded sadly. He knew how Rachel hated to see him leave, but he had no choice. Rachel had another worry too, and it was the reason she wanted privacy more than ever. She feared with a husband in public life that her divorce and remarriage would come back to haunt her. And in the long run, she was right.

On December 5, 1796, Andrew presented himself to Congress. Coming from the newest state, he was closely watched by other congressmen. One of them, Albert Gallatin of Pennsylvania, recorded this first impression of the twenty-nine year old representative.

"He was a tall, lanky, uncouth-looking personage," Gallatin said. "He had a queue down his back tied with an eel-skin . . . and his manners were those of a rough backwoodsman."

But remarks such as this did not bother Andrew Jackson. He was his own man and wasn't about to change his ways for anyone.

Three days after he arrived, George Washington made his farewell address to Congress. John Adams was to be inaugurated as the second president of the United States.

Representative Jackson was not a huge Washington supporter, especially after the passage of the Jay Treaty. The treaty gave the British the right to board and search American ships at sea. Washington felt the treaty was better than war. But Andrew Jackson would have taken the war.

He was also opposed to Washington's Indian policy. He felt it wasn't tough enough when it came to moving the red man from lands whites needed. So when Congress voted to honor the outgoing President with a special celebration, Andrew Jackson was one of only twelve congressmen to vote against it.

In fact, during his short time in the House, Representative Jackson made just one major speech, and it had to do with Indians. He introduced a bill which would repay settlers money spent to fight the Cherokee wars of

1793 in the Cumberland Valley. Those against it said the war was illegal. Jackson's answer in part was:

"The knife and the tomahawk were held over the heads of women and children. It was time to make resistance."

Some of the congressmen weren't convinced because they had never lived on the frontier. Others didn't think it right that the white man kept pushing the Indians off their lands. But Andrew Jackson was looking at it through a frontiersman's eyes. He, his family, and friends all found their lives in danger because of problems with the Indians.

With the support of several powerful politicians, such as James Madison, the bill passed. The settlers were given the money.

Jackson's term ended on March 3, 1797. The entire House of Representatives was up for reelection. Jackson chose not to run again and in a letter to Rachel, told her he'd be coming home to stay.

"With what pleasing hopes I view the future when I shall be restored to your arms, there to spend my days with you, the Dear Companion of my life, never to be separated from you again. . . . I mean to retire from public life."

He returned to Tennessee in May, a hero to the people and more popular than ever. But all he wanted was to be with Rachel at Hunter's Hill. For a short time, it looked as if that was where he'd be.

In July, just two months after returning home, he learned that the Tennessee legislature had appointed him to fill an empty spot in the United States Senate. After hesitating briefly, Jackson felt the call to duty. How could he say no when his state and country called? He wrote his friend Robert Hays:

"Try to amuse Mrs. Jackson. I left her bathed in tears . . . (which) indeed Sir has given me more pain than any event in my life."

Though he went to the Senate full of energy, he found it boring. Andrew always hated to sit still, and it seemed that was all he was doing in the Senate. There were delays, talk, debate, more delays. Nothing seemed to get done.

In April of 1798, he learned that more of the notes he had signed a few years earlier in Philadelphia were due. The man who issued them couldn't pay. In fact, he had gone to jail. That made Andrew totally responsible. He left the Senate and went home to work on his debts.

This was the pattern of the next few years. He worked hard to make Hunter's Hill turn a profit. He even bought a new invention, the cotton gin, which did the work of forty men, separating the seeds from the cotton. His debts were reduced.

His next appointment made him a judge of the Superior Court of Tennessee. He served for four years. He was fair and honest, and won the complete trust of the people. But at the turn of the century, a depression set in. Many men began losing money, Andrew Jackson included. Making ends meet continued to be a major struggle.

In 1802, he became leader of the state militia. It was

the beginning of his official military career. Of course, as long as there was no war, the job did not demand too much of his time. But his men trusted him from the beginning.

Money problems continued. Finally, in the summer of 1804, Andrew felt he had to resign as judge to settle his debts for good. The situation was bad. Andrew was forced to make a very difficult decision.

"Mrs. Jackson," he said to Rachel one night. "I would give anything not to have to tell you this. But we have to move."

Rachel couldn't believe her ears. "Move!" Where? When? Why?"

Andrew shook his head. "We've got to. It's the only way we can get out of debt. I know a man who'll buy Hunter's Hill right now."

Then Andrew told her he wanted to move to a nearby farm he owned. He called it the Hermitage. There was a two-story blockhouse there that he had once hoped to turn into a store. The blockhouse had one huge room downstairs. The floor was made from logs that were shaped as flat as possible. The upstairs had two smaller rooms, and the kitchen was separate from the house.

Rachel listened as Andrew described the place, then quickly agreed.

"If you think it's best, we'll move," she said. "And we'll turn the blockhouse into a real home."

It would be a task. The blockhouse and three small cabins on the farm were not in good condition. Some of the beams were rotting and had to be replaced. Almost all the doors and windows needed repair. Everything was dirty and dusty.

Though she had to leave most of her fine furnishings to the new owner of Hunter's Hill, Rachel Jackson didn't complain. With her husband at her side, she felt she could bear anything.

The sale of Hunter's Hill brought enough for Andrew to finally pay his debts. Rachel worked hard to turn the Hermitage into their new home, while Andrew made plans for his new farm. He had only his military office now, and had the time to begin a new business. It was a business close to his heart, training and raising race horses.

Horses had always been a big part of Andrew's life. He had the skill of a veterinarian and felt he was a keen judge of horses. When he chose a stallion named Truxton to head his stables, he had almost no money. He managed to scrape up the fifteen hundred dollars needed to buy the horse. Truxton was a big bay, beautifully formed, with white hind feet.

"With the right training, this horse can be a champion," Jackson told his friends. "I'm staking everything on it."

He was correct. Truxton was a champion and a winner. Andrew bet heavily on the bay's first races and won. He was able to buy more horses. People began to pay a lot of money to have Jackson's horses father colts for them.

By the spring of 1806, Truxton had run several races against Captain Joseph Erwin's horse, Ploughboy. Erwin

*Horses had always been a big part of Andrew's life.*

was a wealthy Nashville sportsman who loved to bet and loved to win. A great deal of money was bet on the first race. But at the last moment, Ploughboy was withdrawn. Erwin had to pay a forfeit to Jackson in notes. But anger ran high, and there was even talk that the whole thing was fixed.

"By God," Jackson roared. "If that's what people think, we'll race them again!"

A second race was arranged. But the day before the race, Truxton hurt a thigh in practice. Some of Andrew's

82

friends thought he should pull Truxton out of the race. Andrew walked over to his horse. He spoke softly in its ears. As people who knew him said, when Andrew Jackson spoke to a horse he looked in its eyes, as he looked at men.

"What are you going to do, Mr. Jackson?" one of the trainers asked. Several others gathered around, waiting for an answer.

"I'm going to run him," Jackson said.

"But the horse is lame," said another.

"Not that lame. Truxton will run."

Andrew's judgment was sound. The big stallion was never better. He whipped Ploughboy in every heat, winning the final race by sixty yards. Huge amounts of money changed hands. And, as usual, when it was over, the losers were angry.

Captain Erwin's son-in-law, Charles Dickinson, began talking without thinking. In his anger he raised a question about Andrew's marriage to Rachel, saying that Jackson had wed an already-married woman.

Tempers flared and the war of words continued. Suddenly, it was more than words. The two men agreed to a duel. Dueling was a way that gentlemen of the time supposedly settled arguments with their honor intact. In a duel, opponents faced each other with pistols and had one shot each. Sometimes they only fired into the air. No one was hurt, and the men saved their honor. But at other times, they shot to kill.

Andrew might have settled for a bullet in the air, but he soon heard that Dickinson had vowed to kill him.

He also knew that Dickinson was a crack shot, an expert marksman. Jackson, while good, was no expert. And although Rachel knew and liked Charles Dickinson's pregnant wife, she also knew not to interfere with her husband's personal affairs.

The two men met on May 30, 1806.

They had traveled across the border into Kentucky to a spot along the Red River near Harrison's Mills. Charles Dickinson was so sure he would win that he told his wife he'd be home by the next evening. He also offered to wager anyone that he would kill Jackson with his first shot.

It was a warm day as Andrew Jackson rode over the old Kentucky road. It was the same road he had traveled fifteen years earlier when he helped Rachel Robards leave her husband's home. He wondered if he would ever travel it again.

The duel was to be fought at a distance of twenty-four feet. Facing each other, the two men would keep their pistols facing downward. At the word "FIRE," they could shoot as quickly as they pleased. Each had one shot. If one man fired before the command, the other's assistant, or second, would shoot the man down.

"I will not compete with him for first shot," Jackson had told his friends. "I'll probably be hit, maybe badly, but by God I'll find a way to get my shot off! That you can believe."

The two men met on the bank of the Red River. General Thomas Overton, brother of John Overton, was Jackson's chief second, while Dr. Hanson Catlett assisted

Dickinson. They would use Jackson's pistols, single-shot dueling pistols with nine-inch barrels. They were charged with one-ounce balls of seventy caliber.

It was almost deathly quiet as the two men took their positions. Jackson was wearing a dark blue frock coat and blue trousers. Dickinson had a shorter coat, also blue, but with gray trousers. One of the buttons on Jackson's type of coat normally lay directly over the heart. That was the spot where Dickinson planned to aim.

"Gentleman, are you ready?" General Overton asked.

"Yes, sir," said Andrew

"Ready," Dickinson answered.

"*Fere!*" General Overton shouted, in an Irish accent from the old country.

In an instant, Charles Dickinson raised his pistol and fired. A whisk of dust could be seen rising from Jackson's coat, and his left hand clutched at his chest. For a second he thought he would fall. He had a serious wound, maybe one that would kill him. Then, slowly, he raised his pistol.

Dickinson's mouth dropped open in shock. *Could he have missed?* General Overton quickly commanded him back to his mark. All Charles Dickinson could do was fold his arms and wait. No one would ever know what was going through his mind at that moment.

Andrew aimed the pistol, drew back the hammer, aimed again and . . . fired! Dickinson swayed, then fell to the ground.

As Dickinson's second rushed to his aid, Andrew

*In an instant, Charles Dickenson raised his pistol and fired.*

Jackson calmly walked to his horse. But when John Overton reached him, he saw that Andrew's left boot was filled with blood.

"I believe he pinked me," Jackson said, slowly, "but I don't want those people to know."

In truth, Dickinson's aim had been perfect. He hit the button on Jackson's coat just as he'd planned. But because Jackson was so thin, the coat hung loosely, and the button was not over his heart, but to the left of it. That's where the bullet had lodged.

Dickinson was hit in the abdomen. He hung on in

pain through the night, but died the next morning. To make his final minutes more peaceful, his friends told him that Jackson was also dying. But as the strong-willed Jackson had told John Overton:

"I should have hit him even if he had shot me through the brain."

Upon hearing the news of Dickinson's death and that Andrew had lived, Rachel Jackson's first thought was:

"Oh, God, have pity on the poor wife, and pity on the babe in her womb."

# CHAPTER NINE

# The War Years

Andrew Jackson's wound healed slowly. The bullet was too close to his heart to be removed. In later years, the wound would cause his lung to bleed, and Andrew would remember that morning on the banks of the Red River. His enemies, however, never knew how serious the injury was. They thought he was cruel to shoot back at Dickinson.

Yes, Jackson had shot to kill, just as Dickinson had. And although many people felt dueling was brutal and old fashioned, Andrew Jackson had only followed the rules. He wasn't proud of having killed a man, but he felt he had done what was right.

During the next few years, Andrew took it easy. He spent more time at home with Rachel and threw his energy into his businesses. The Hermitage bustled with activity. Visits from nieces and nephews from Rachel's large family brightened up their lives. And when Rachel's brother Sam died, the Jacksons took in his two sons, to raise and educate them.

In December of 1809, Rachel was called to the home of another brother, Severn Donelson. His wife was expecting a baby, but she was in poor health and the family was worried. Rachel went there at a gallop. She reached her brother's house in time to help in the unexpected birth of twin boys.

With the new twins, there would now be four very young children in Severn Donelson's house. His wife was frail and sickly. Donelson feared she could not care for them. When he told Rachel his fears, she had an idea.

"Can I take the second twin home?" she asked. "Mr. Jackson and I will be very good to him. He loves Sam's boys and this baby will be like our very own."

Severn Donelson went to ask his wife. When he returned to his sister, he smiled and nodded.

"Oh, brother " Rachel Jackson said. "You don't know how very happy you have just made me."

When Rachel returned to the Hermitage in January of 1810, she was carrying a small bundle. When she saw Andrew, she couldn't contain her joy.

"We have a baby, Mr. Jackson," she cried. "We have a baby of our very own!"

Andrew was surprised, but happy. In fact, he was so pleased that he immediately gave the boy his own name: Andrew Jackson, Jr. The boy was accepted as his son and heir. As soon as they could, the Jacksons legally adopted the boy. For the first time Rachel felt as if their life together was complete.

By 1811, Jackson had lost some of his enthusiasm for the world of finance. He sold shares he had in several stores, and even parted with his old favorite, the Clover Bottom Race Track. He was getting more interested in politics again. Tension between America and England was growing.

Britain wanted to stop its former colony from trading abroad. The powerful British Navy stopped American ships and often kidnapped the sailors. To many, including Andrew Jackson, war seemed liked the only way to solve the problem.

Andrew had opposed President Thomas Jefferson's policies toward England as early as 1808. Jefferson wanted to keep the peace, while Jackson felt America should stand up to Britain. In the 1808 election, he supported James Monroe over James Madison for the same reason. But Madison was elected the fourth president of the country. Andrew was now a general in the state militia. Troubles with England were getting worse and worse. He was ready to lead his troops into battle.

"My only pride is that my soldiers have confidence in me," he said, "and in the event of war I will lead them to victory. Should we be blest with peace I will resign my military office and spend my days in the sweet calm of rural retirement."

But everyone was talking about war in the spring of 1812. The eastern states were against a war. But the West had a group of angry young men in Congress who wanted to fight. Led by Henry Clay of Kentucky and John C. Calhoun of South Carolina, these "war hawks" felt the British had gone too far. American's honor had to be won back.

Finally, on June 18, the House of Representatives voted 79-49. America was at war with England!

Within days, General Andrew Jackson offered his services to President Madison. He had twenty-five hundred men of the Tennessee militia trained and ready to go to war immediately. He was just awaiting orders. But none came.

The general could only wait for news while the American army marched into Canada. One reason the United States had declared war was to free Canada from England's rule. But the first trip north of the border was a failure. The troops were beaten, and American troops never had a real chance of victory in Canada again.

Through it all, Jackson waited. When an order finally came to Tennessee in October it wasn't to the general, but to Governor Blount. Blount was asked to lead fifteen hundred men to join General Wilkinson at New Orleans. For some reason, Congress was ignoring Jackson. But Governor Blount had the right to choose a commander. He quickly picked Andrew Jackson.

The volunteers came from everywhere. More than twenty-five hundred men showed up in Nashville by December 10. General Jackson had taken out a personal loan of more than fifteen hundred dollars to help equip his men. At the general's suggestion, most of the men wore blue or brown hunting coats, buckskin hunting shirts, and dark socks and pants.

Suddenly, Nashville was hit by freezing cold. It was so cold that even the Cumberland River froze over. That happened only four or five times every hundred years!

The Tennessee Militia marched anyway. It took them thirty-nine days to reach their goal. Andrew Jackson never tired. He led his men through the cold and helped them brave the other dangers in traveling the frontier. Only three men could not finish the march.

But the long and difficult journey turned out to be for nothing. Jackson was ordered to set up camp outside Natchez and await further orders. It took nearly a month for the orders to come. The orders both surprised and angered Andrew Jackson.

"The orders say to dismiss my men," he said with shock. "Just like that. We're not needed."

The Tennessee volunteers had been abandoned. There was no pay, no food, no transportation, no medicine for the sick. The men looked to their leader.

"We'll make it home, men," he told them. "We'll make it home if I have to pay for the food myself. Even if we have to eat our horses along the way, we'll make it."

Then he wrote his wife to tell her of the disaster. He signed the letter fondly, saying:

"Kiss my little Andrew for me and tell him his papa is coming home."

And home they went. General Jackson walked with his troops the entire way. Only sick soldiers rode horseback. The men couldn't believe the way their general held up during the long march. He walked straight and tall, moving briskly day after day, for hours at a time. When the men were tired, he cheered them on. When they were cold and hungry, he spurred them forward with tales of warm homes and full bellies. When they got angry or depressed, he smiled and joked with them. He was their strength, their rock. Younger men marveled at his energy, and pushed to keep up with him. His toughness and will impressed them all.

"The general is as tough as this piece of hickory," said one soldier, holding up a walking stick he had made out of hard hickory wood.

"He sure is," added another. "There's nobody tougher."

And as the march continued, the name spread. Someone added an "old" before the hickory. By the time the weary soldiers marched into the Cumberland Valley, Andrew Jackson had a nickname that would stick: Old Hickory.

The militia returned as heroes. But that wasn't enough for Andrew Jackson. He immediately volunteered his troops to help with the war in Canada. But again the same answer came from the nation's capitol.

"We don't need you!"

Jackson had another urgent problem. He had borrowed heavily to help his troops. At first Congress made no move to help him. Once again trouble with money threatened to ruin Andrew Jackson. He steeled himself for the worst. But suddenly, help came from a newfound friend.

Thomas Hart Benton was a young lawyer who had become a trusted aide to Jackson on the march. Hearing of Jackson's troubles, Benton said:

"Let me get in touch with a congressman I know. He owes me a favor."

Sure enough, through Benton's efforts, Congress decided to repay Jackson's expenses. It seemed that a genuine friendship had grown between Benton and Jackson. But then an unexpected event destroyed the friendship, and almost ended Jackson's military career . . . and his life!

It had started on the march. Benton's younger brother, Jesse, had argued with Major William Carroll, one of Jackson's friends. At first, the two men merely exchanged insults. But one thing led to another. Before long the two younger men talked of fighting a duel. Carroll asked General Jackson to be one of his seconds.

"I'm too old for that," Jackson replied quickly. "Besides, your argument is no cause for a duel. Get together and talk things over."

It was good advice, but unfortunately, it fell on deaf ears. The duel was held and Jackson agreed to assist Billy Carroll. Jesse Benton got only a minor injury. But the wound was in his buttocks. That made the duel more of a bad joke than anything else. Both Benton and Carroll felt embarrassed.

Thomas Hart Benton, however, was angry with Jackson for taking part in it. He began siding with his brother against the general. More people joined the argument. Soon there were rumors and stories and tall tales being told on both sides. It reached a point where an angry Jackson even threatened to horsewhip Thomas Benton the next time he saw him.

Finally, on the morning of September 4, 1813, the Benton brothers came to Nashville.

"We went to the City Hotel, instead of the Nashville Inn," Thomas Benton revealed, "because we knew the general and his friends were often at the Inn and we didn't want any problems."

Yet each of the Bentons wore two pistols. Sure enough, Andrew Jackson arrived at the Inn about the same time the two brothers entered the lobby of the City Hotel. Andrew was with two close friends, John Coffee and Stockley Hays. A short time later, Jackson and Coffee went to the post office. When they came back, they spotted Thomas Hart Benton standing in the doorway of the City Hotel.

General Jackson had his riding whip with him. He began to threaten Benton with it.

"Defend yourself, you rascal," he shouted.

Benton reached for his pistol, but Jackson drew his out first. He backed Benton into the corridor of the hotel. But he didn't see Jesse Benton, who came through a doorway behind him at that very moment. Seeing Jackson holding a gun on his brother, Jesse Benton drew his own weapon and fired. Jackson fell forward, his own gun firing wildly.

John Coffee swung into action. He went to club Thomas Benton with his pistol. In the scuffle, Benton fell backwards down a flight of stairs. Stockley Hays had run to the scene. He rushed at Jesse Benton with his sword raised. By then, people were coming from every direction. It was a real brawl between men who should never have been enemies.

Andrew Jackson was the most seriously hurt. Blood gushed from his left shoulder. Doctors tried to stop the flow of blood, but it was difficult. His pulse was very weak, his color bad. Some people thought this was the end for Old Hickory.

News of the shooting spread quickly. The crowds gathered. Some of the general's friends vowed revenge, and the Bentons left town quickly. Andrew was carried to an empty room in the hotel. A number of the doctors wanted to cut off his injured arm. Hearing this from the doctors, Jackson raised his head from the pillow. He spoke with great effort, but with equal finality.

"I'll keep my arm," he ordered.

The doctors listened.

"If he makes it through the night he's got a chance," one said.

"The general is going to be a sick man for a long time, even if he makes it," said another.

The vigil continued. Andrew was still alive in the morning. Rachel was by his side by then, holding his hand and talking to him.

"You must live," she said, over and over again. "We all love you and need you."

Perhaps Rachel's words gave him strength for Andrew slowly began to heal. Before long, he was strong enough to go home. At the Hermitage, his recovery continued. The bullet was still lodged in his left shoulder, and his arm would never be the same. But at least he would live.

Two weeks passed. Jackson lay in bed. He felt angry that he had let the whole thing happen. Now he was stuck in bed because of it. Then, on September 18, he had a visitor. It was his friend, John Coffee. The news wasn't good.

"There's been a massacre," Coffee told Jackson. "The Creek Indians are on the warpath. A chief named Red Eagle is leading them. They attacked Fort Mims near Mobile Bay."

"How many killed?" asked Jackson from his bed.

"About two hundred and fifty, nearly everyone in the fort."

Jackson winced. He knew too well about Indian attacks, and Mobile Bay in the Mississippi Territory wasn't that far from Nashville. Coffee told him that the people were frightened. What if the Indians' unrest spread? They could all be threatened. Coffee was already forming a cavalry and waiting for federal or state approval to go after Red Eagle. There was just one problem.

"The men want you to lead them," Coffee said.

Before Andrew could answer, Rachel spoke out.

"But he can't. Don't you see how sick he is? His wound hasn't had proper time to heal."

Coffee looked away. He knew he was asking a great deal. He could see how Mrs. Jackson felt about the request. But then the general raised his right hand.

"You tell the men their general is coming," Andrew said, the strength suddenly returning to his voice. "No shoulder wound is going to keep me from serving my country."

Rachel protested, but Andrew stopped her with a look.

"My decision is final," he said.

*The Creek Indians are on the warpath.*

That night Andrew wrote a letter to Governor Blount. "The health of your general is restored. He will command in person."

Twenty-five hundred men would march to the Mississippi Territory. They would leave in nine days. That was all the time Andrew had to get back on his feet and find the strength to lead his troops into battle.

He forced himself out of bed. Each day he tried to do a little more, walking slowly around his room, then on the grounds. Finally, he got on his horse and took short rides around the Hermitage. He also began getting reports telling him what had happened at Fort Mims.

The Indian Chief called Red Eagle had an unusual past. He was born with the name William Weatherford. His father was a trader from Scotland, and his mother a part Creek Indian. Their children had to decide in which world they wanted to belong. One son, John Weatherford, chose the white race, and lived a quiet life. But the other, William, chose to be a Creek. In time he took the name Red Eagle.

Not many white people had heard of Red Eagle until war with England began in 1812. But two years earlier, the young Indian had met the great chief Tecumseh. The meeting changed Red Eagle's life.

Tecumseh had a plan that would unite all the Indian tribes, from the Great Lakes in the North to the Gulf of Mexico in the South. He felt this was the only way the red man could stop the white man from taking their lands. Indians had been pushed further and further West for years now, and Tecumseh saw no end to it. But his plan failed because new treaties temporarily satisfied some of the tribes. Tecumseh tried to unite the tribes again a year later. This time he made a big impression on thirty-one year old Red Eagle. Red Eagle was convinced his people had to fight for their land.

The Indians had been quiet for a while. General William Henry Harrison had defeated a large Indian force led by Tecumseh's brother, The Prophet, at the battle of Tippecanoe. It seemed to slow the Indians down. Then the United States declared war on England.

The British quickly got the Indians to fight on their side. They gave them weapons and other goods. Before long, Red Eagle had his braves putting on the war paint once again. For his first target he picked the largest stockade in the Mississippi region, Fort Mims. News of the massacre spread quickly. Americans up and down the river feared for their lives.

So, as Andrew Jackson continued to build up his strength, he learned as much as he could about the man called Red Eagle. The more information the general had, the easier it would be to do battle with him.

General Jackson's troops had already moved on to Fayetteville, some eighty miles from Nashville. Now the men waited for their leader to arrive.

"Do you think he'll make it?" one soldier asked.

"Don't know," said another. "That bullet he took nearly killed him."

"Gen'l Jackson will be here," a third said. "He's the toughest man I know."

So they waited. Then on October 7, just a week after

100

he began walking, Andrew Jackson rode into camp. His left arm was in a sling, but he sat tall in the saddle. The men cheered wildly. Old Hickory hadn't let them down. Now they could head south and take care of Red Eagle. They had their leader back.

Colonel Coffee and his cavalry had already moved on to Creek territory. Jackson and his soldiers planned to join them at Ditto's Landing on the Tennessee River just below Huntsville.

Jackson didn't bring his troops south just to wander around looking for Indians. After joining Coffee they moved twenty-four miles along the Tennessee River to its southern tip. There, they built a stockade called Fort Deposit. They would store most of their supplies in the heavy log structure.

Then they moved across the Raccoon Mountains and built a second stockade. Supplies were already low, but, General Jackson was ready to act. Though the men were hungry, getting only a handful of Indian corn to eat, they pushed on, searching for the Creeks.

On November 3, 1813, they came across a Creek Village with nearly two hundred braves. Jackson sent Coffee in with one thousand men. The Americans poured it on. Davy Crockett, the famous frontiersman, who would later die fighting for Texas at the Alamo, was part of Jackson's army. As he put it:

"We shot them like dogs."

It was, indeed, a one-sided battle. Not a single Creek warrior escaped and some eighty-four women and children were captured. Only five of Coffee's men were killed and forty-one were wounded.

"We have retaliated for Fort Mims," Jackson wrote.

Though he was a tough commander who always hit his enemies with full force, there was a soft side to Andrew Jackson. After the battle, he noticed a small Creek boy, about three years old, among the prisoners. The boy's parents were dead and the other Creek women refused to care for him.

"Kill him, too," they said.

Hearing that, General Jackson dismounted and went to the boy. He ordered some brown sugar mixed with water and tenderly held the boy until he drank some of the sweet mixture. He looked again at the small boy, then thought of Andrew, Jr., back at the Hermitage. He called an aide over.

"Bring this boy to Huntsville," he commanded. "And take good care of him. When you get there, make arrangements for him to be taken to my home. Mrs. Jackson will care for him there."

That night, he wrote Rachel about the boy. He called him Lincoyer, and said he wanted to raise him at the Hermitage. The kind Mrs. Jackson welcomed Lincoyer as one of her own.

Six days later a second battle took place outside the town of Talladega. The site was some thirty miles south of the first battle, across the Coosa River. Jackson had been told that Red Eagle had a thousand Indian braves there. The general had fallen sick. He felt weak. But he willed himself to go on and led his weary and hungry men to the outskirts of the town.

Figuring the Indians were waiting for him, Jackson sent three mounted teams in, hoping to draw an Indian attack. Sure enough, the Creeks took the bait. When the cavalrymen seemed to retreat, the Indians came after them. They ran straight into the rest of Jackson's men.

When the Indians charged out after the mounted teams, they expected an easy victory. But Jackson had placed the rest of his men in a half circle. Even though they were in the open, Jackson had spread his men wide enough. When the ends of the half circle closed together, the Indians were surrounded.

It was a brutal scene. The rifle shots made a deafening roar, and the smoke from the powder rose in a slow cloud. But even worse were the screams, as the Creek Indians fell dead and dying all around. The battle ended with three hundred Creeks killed. Only fifteen American soldiers died in the battle.

Now Red Eagle had suffered two bad defeats within six days. General Jackson might have followed him and ended it right there. But the lack of food was too great a problem, especially for the wounded. There was just no way to get food supplies quickly on the frontier.

So the general pulled his men back to Fort Deposit, hoping that fresh supplies had arrived. But when the army reached the stockade, Andrew found that food and medicine had not arrived.

Waiting was the worst part. Jackson hated it. But without food he had no choice. Now some of the men were getting restless. They wanted to go home. Some had already spent their required year in military service. Others were just plain hungry. More than once, the general had to convince the men to stay. If talking didn't work, he'd threaten to shoot them. No one was about to desert Andrew Jackson.

Then new recruits arrived, so some of the men could go home. By mid January of 1814, Jackson felt it was time for a final push. The Americans headed for a horseshoe shaped bend in the Tallapoosa River. The Creeks were camped there. Water protected them on three sides and the forest lay behind them.

"There are about eight hundred braves and three hundred women and children in the camp," the general told his fellow officers. "Red Eagle is leading them. If we do this right, perhaps we can end this fight once and for all."

It was the Indians who attacked first. But Jackson was ready and his men pushed the Indians back to their camp. If he had more guns and bullets, Jackson might have attacked the camp right away. But he had to wait. For the next weeks, he had to fight minor battles and wait for reinforcements.

Finally, on March 27, General Jackson felt his time had come. He had two thousand men at the Horseshoe Bend. Would this be the final battle with the Creeks and Red Eagle?

First Jackson surrounded the Horseshoe. Then, he sent some of his soldiers to swim across the river and carry off the Creek canoes. That cut off one major escape

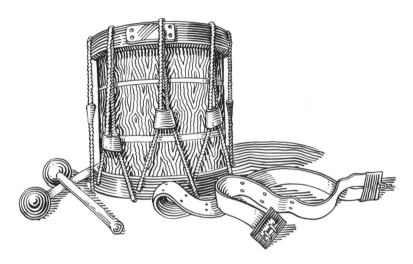

*A roll of drums signaled the attack.*

route. Jackson then allowed the Creek women and children to cross the river to safety.

A roll of drums at about twelve thirty in the afternoon signaled the attack. Jackson's soldiers charged. The fighting was fierce. At one point in the battle, Jackson offered to protect any Indian who would surrender. None did. By nighttime, only a small band of red men fought on. Another offer to surrender was flatly refused.

The battle continued until just past dusk. Then the last of the Indians were overrun. Almost five hundred and fifty-seven Creeks lay dead inside the Horseshoe. Another two hundred bodies floated in the river. Jackson's forces lost just forty-nine men, with another one hundred and fifty-seven wounded. Old Hickory had broken the heart and spirit of the Creek nation. After the battle, the tall general said he had but two regrets.

"Two or three women and children were killed by accident," he said. "I didn't want that. And when we moved in, we found that Red Eagle wasn't there. He hadn't been there for the entire battle."

Jackson felt that Red Eagle had to be killed or captured to truly end the Indian uprising. He moved his troops south to the Creek Holy Land. The few Indians who had fled there scattered. The Americans then raised their flag, and what had once been Fort Toulous was renamed Fort Jackson. In the next few days, most of the Creek leaders surrendered to the Americans.

Several days later, a tall, light-skinned Indian walked slowly into the post. He was bare to the waist. He wore only tattered buckskin pants and threadbare moccasins. He was unarmed. He walked up to General Jackson's tent. When Old Hickory came out, the Indian surprised everyone.

"I am Bill Weatherford," he said. It was Red Eagle himself.

Jackson was astonished, and for a split second he hated the man standing before him.

"How dare you show yourself at my tent after having murdered women and children at Fort Mims!"

But the Indian leader was alone and unarmed. Jackson took him inside his tent. The man called Red Eagle spoke.

"I have come to give myself up. I can oppose you no longer. I know I have done you much injury. I should have done you more, but my warriors are dead. Now I am in your power. Dispose of me as you please."

Andrew Jackson looked at the tall man before him. Weatherford had come in on his own. He stood before him still proud, not a bit sorry for what he had done. Nor did he beg for mercy. Despite the death and destruction Red Eagle had caused, Jackson had respect for the man.

"You are not in my power," the general replied. "I had ordered you brought before me in chains, yet you have come on your own. You now see my camp and my soldiers. If you want to continue your battle against me, return to lead your warriors."

"I cannot lead the dead," Weatherford said. "and I ask nothing for myself. I only beg you to send for our women and children and help them. They have never done you any harm. Then, if the white people want it, you can kill me."

Jackson looked Weatherford straight in the eye. He thought of the little Indian boy, Lincoyer, whom he had sent to the Hermitage. Perhaps the time for hatred was over. He poured Weatherford a drink.

"I will help your women and children," he said. "As for you . . . you are free to go."

The general put out his hand. Red Eagle grasped it. He then turned and left the tent. When he left the camp, the soldiers couldn't believe it. But General Jackson had made his decision.

So Bill Weatherford, the great warrior Red Eagle, vanished into the wilderness, and from history. That night, Jackson sat down at his writing table, took out his quill pen and inkwell, and wrote about the man he defeated.

"Weatherford was the greatest of the Barbarian world. He possessed all the manliness of sentiment, all the heroism of soul. You have seen his speech to General Jackson, . . . but you could not see his looks and gestures, the modesty and yet the firmness that were in them."

Respect, from one great warrior to another. Yet Andrew Jackson couldn't relax for long. Yes, the Creek war was over, but there was still the matter of the British. And now there was no way Congress could deny him a command. He had earned it.

# CHAPTER TEN

# The Battle of New Orleans

Andrew Jackson returned to the Cumberland a hero. Rachel and Andrew, Jr., met him at Huntsville to bring him home. Crowds cheered him everywhere. Here, at last, was a general who would stop at nothing less than total victory. As his friend, John Overton, said to him:

"I can sense the feeling of the people. Your standing is as high as any man in America."

But Old Hickory wasn't finished, not by a long shot. He was only going home for a short rest. On May 28, 1814, he was named a major-general in the United States Army, commanding the seventh military district. That district included Tennessee, Louisiana, and the Mississippi Territory.

When they gave him the command, the War Department didn't think there would be much more fighting in the South. They even chose other men to work out a peace treaty with the Creeks. But Old Hickory wouldn't hear of it.

"I'm the only one who is going to make the treaty with the Creeks," he told friends. "Not some general who was sitting in an office while we were fighting at Horseshoe Bend."

Jackson quickly put his words into action. Using all the powers he could, he convinced the War Department that he was the man to make the peace treaty. At the same time, he promised that if there were any more problems with the British in the South they would come to a quick end.

Peace talks would be held at the newly named Fort Jackson. Old Hickory gave the Creek chiefs an invitation they couldn't refuse: those who didn't show up would be destroyed.

The chiefs who came mirrored the troubles of their people. They were thin, gaunt-looking, and obviously hungry. The war had forced them to move around so much that there were no crops, no harvest of corn for them to eat. They were in serious trouble and General Jackson knew it.

His terms were harsh. The Indians already had a name for him. It was Sharp Knife. He was a hard man and he drove a hard bargain with the Indians. The Creeks would have to give up twenty-three million acres of land, part of it in Georgia, and more than half of what became Alabama. They would lose more than half their total land.

"The cost of the war you started must be paid," Jackson told them. "The territory you must leave leads the path that Tecumseh trod. That path must be stopped. Your people must also be separated from Spain and Britain, who were your allies against us. Until this is done, your nation cannot expect happiness."

He added that those who signed would be regarded as friends; those who didn't, as enemies. Though the terms tore the very hearts from the Indians, they had no choice. They signed the treaty on August 9, 1814. Even Creeks who were friendly to the Americans and aided Jackson in his battle with Red Eagle had to agree to the treaty.

Many called Andrew Jackson a hero all over again. Some, however, felt the treaty was unfair, and much too harsh. But the tall general was looking to the future. He knew that more white men were coming. They would continue to come. Instead of taking the lands away bit by bit, as so many previous treaties had done, this treaty cleared out a huge area and moved the Indians west. And perhaps, in the long run, that was the kinder way to do it. Yet he still wrote these words to Rachel, showing he did not enjoy this business.

"A disagreeable business was done. I know your humanity would feel for them."

Then there were the British. A few months before war had been declared in 1812, Andrew Jackson had written:

"We are going to fight for the reestablishment of our national character."

But it hadn't exactly worked out that way. The winter before the war had been very harsh. There were many major crop failures, food prices went sky high, people were hungry and out of work. There were less than seven thousand men in the regular army. The officers weren't skilled in the ways of war. Few people volunteered for the army.

The country was not well prepared for a war with a battle-ready country such as England. The Americans were lucky since the British were busy fighting the French at the same time. That way, they couldn't concentrate all their energies across the ocean.

Still, many Americans thought the war would be short and easy. Some figured on an easy march into Canada, followed by a quick peace. But it didn't work out that way. Attempts to march into Canada ended in failure and defeat.

In August of 1812, the city of Detroit fell to the British. Then there were several other defeats in the Northeast. For the next year or so, the war went back and forth, though American ships won a surprising number of victories at sea. Then in 1814, the British defeated the French. They were now free to send more troops across the Atlantic.

Once again things went badly for the Americans. The British began to feel hopeful. They had long dreamed of getting back some of the territory they had lost in the Revolution. On August 24, 1814, just several weeks after Andrew Jackson signed his peace treaty with the Creeks, British troops overran Washington, D.C. They burned several government buildings, including the White House. President James Madison and his family were forced to flee the city.

It was beginning to look more like a no-win situation. The Americans stopped the British at Baltimore.

*A large number of British boats were arriving in Florida.*

Then another British force was defeated further north. Peace talks were already underway in Belgium. By now, many Americans were exhausted by the war. Some of the states in the Northeast were even talking of giving in.

Andrew Jackson had returned to Mobile, Alabama, on August 22, just two days before Washington fell to the British. He then learned that a large number of British boats were arriving in Spanish-controlled Florida. The General knew the British wanted to take New Orleans and set up a strong southern base.

The question was how to stop them. At the end of November, General Jackson made his first visit to New Orleans. He found a city living in fear. There were very few guns and little money. Jackson made a dramatic speech, pledging to save the city from the British.

But, as usual, Andrew Jackson had his own, tough methods. Many of the citizens didn't like it.

"I feel it necessary to declare martial law in the city until the crisis is over," he said. "That means all firearms of any kind must be turned in."

Most of the people went along with the order. They trusted Old Hickory and they were scared. But one group that didn't turn in its guns was the Baratarians, a bunch of men who lived in a hide-out near Lake Barataria, southwest of the city. The Baratarians were pirates led by a man named Jean Lafitte. They raided and robbed ships, often selling their stolen goods in New Orleans.

The British contacted Jean Lafitte first. They asked for his help in New Orleans. But the pirate chief felt closer ties to the Americans. He offered his services to General Jackson. At first, Jackson refused. But later, when he learned that Lafitte and his pirates were skilled fighters on land, he took them as allies.

The first battle for New Orleans was fought at sea, on December 14, 1814. The British fleet sailed onto Lake Borgne to confront American ships. The smaller American boats kept the British ships busy at first. But the odds were too great. Some forty-five English gunboats finally defeated the five American ships after an hour of savage fighting.

"I had not counted on this," Jackson said, when told the grim news. "Now the northern route to the city is wide open. I wonder if the British are clever enough to take advantage of it."

"What happens next, general?" an aide asked.

"Perhaps it's time we showed our English guests just how we can fight," said Jackson.

The British force of some ten thousand men was commanded by Sir Edward Pakenham. Pakenham's brother-in-law was the Duke of Wellington, the most popular war hero in England. On December 22, Pakenham led the first British troops ashore to the swampy land southeast of New Orleans. They marched to a nearby sugar plantation and set up camp.

It was a cold and rainy night. General Jackson hadn't been well. He had a fever. He also was bleeding inside from the bullet left in his chest by the Dickinson duel. But when he received reports of the new British camp, he knew he had to act.

"We'll attack immediately, tonight," he told his staff, catching many of them by surprise.

"Why so quickly?" one asked.

"It's the British code of warfare," Jackson explained. "They don't normally fight at night. We can take them by surprise."

Sick as he was, Jackson led two thousand troops toward the British camp. He also ordered a gunboat up the river where its guns could reach the camp. The attack was a complete surprise. Many of the British were sleeping in their tents. But they grabbed their rifles and fought back.

The night was filled with flashes of powder and the constant booming of gunfire. The cannon from the gunboat also reached the camp. The loud explosions rang in the soldiers' ears.

The British fought hard, but they hadn't expected a group of screaming, determined fighters. Wars weren't fought this way in Europe. It might have been an even greater victory, but suddenly a dense fog fell, and the Americans were forced to withdraw.

"All right, men," Jackson said later to his officers. "We've given them a taste of what they are up against. Now we've got to prepare again, because this time they'll make a major attack."

The general led his entire force to the Rodriguez Canal, a dried-out ditch that connected the river and the swamp. It was a natural fort. With the swamp on the left and river on the right, Old Hickory hoped the British would be forced to attack from straight ahead.

He ordered strong barricades built. Americans would fire on the British force from behind the barricades. He also counted on the English using their tried and true European battle methods. That meant sending their troops, marching in lines, straight at the enemy.

To build the barricades, the men worked twenty-four hours a day. One group rested, while another group worked. General Jackson was always with his men. He didn't sleep. He supervised everything. He even ate in the saddle. And he kept encouraging his men.

"Keep working. We're almost done," he'd say. "The British have never met the likes of us before. They think it will be easy, but we'll have a big surprise ready for them."

Pakenham's men attacked right before Christmas, but it wasn't with full force. It was as if they were just testing the Americans. The real attack came on January 8, 1815. The English sent their full force of ten thousand men against Andrew Jackson and his five thousand soldiers.

A thick fog hung heavy over the swamp that morning. The English commander felt it would be perfect cover for his troops. They marched in tight lines, as they had in Europe, one column after another. Their drummers and bagpipers set the pace of the march. To General Jackson and his men, it must have sounded more like a parade than a battle march.

But the men waiting to meet the British weren't scared. They were an interesting mixture. There were frontiersmen from Kentucky and Tennessee, black men who used to be slaves, and Jean Lafitte and his band of pirates. All had faced danger and death many times in their lives. They could shoot too. If nothing else, all Andrew Jackson's men could handle a rifle.

Jackson and his men strained to see through the fog. If it didn't lift, they might not see the British until they were right in front of them. If that happened, the British might be able to overpower them. But suddenly a wind arose out of nowhere. It began to blow the fog away.

The wind unmasked the British troops. General Jackson, sitting astride his horse, could see the tight columns some six hundred and fifty yards away. The American rifles only reached targets four hundred yards away.

"Not yet, men," he hollered. "Hold your fire until they get closer."

Then he took a long look at their uniforms. The

British soldiers wore bright red coats with white cross plates across the middle of their chests. "My God," he thought. "It's a perfect target."

"Aim for the cross plates, men," he hollered, spreading the word up and down the line. "Right above the cross plates."

At five hundred yards, the cannon began firing. The large cannonballs caused the British to close ranks even more. But the thick smoke from the cannon was doing the same thing the fog had done. It was covering the targets.

"Stop the cannon," Jackson shouted. "Stop them!"

Now the British were about three hundred yards away. They started to run toward the American lines. Every man on Jackson's line aimed his rifle at the breast plate of a redcoat. This was just the position Andrew Jackson wanted, just the way he hoped it would happen.

"Fire!" he yelled. The order was echoed up and down the line.

What happened in the next few minutes was a chilling sight. The American marksmen mowed down the British soldiers as if they were targets in a shooting gallery. The redcoats fell in heaps. Those behind had to climb over the bodies in order to advance. Most of the redcoats were shot before they could move much further.

General Jackson rode behind the front line, directing the battle from all sides. He ignored the rifle fire all around him. Like most commanders of the day, he fought close by his men. Sir Edward Pakenham, the British leader, felt the same way. He, too, moved forward with his men.

*At five hundred yards, the cannon began firing.*

And Pakenham, too, like many of his men, fell dead, hit three times by the sharpshooting Americans.

A number of other top British officers were killed. One who survived remembered the scene well:

"Never before had British veterans quailed," he said. "But it would be silly to deny that they did so now. That leaden torrent no man on earth could face. I had seen battlefields in Spain and in the East, but nowhere such a scene as this."

And General Jackson, watching his men in action, later wrote that his riflemen fired "with a briskness of which there have been but few instances, perhaps in any country."

Fire! Load! Aim! Fire! Those commands could be heard over and over. The Americans reloaded and fired, reloaded and fired. And the British continued to fall. Finally, it was over. Some of the British fell back. Others stumbled forward with their hands in the air.

"I'll never forget the sight," Jackson said, "of more than five hundred Britons emerging from the heaps of their dead comrades, all over the plain, rising up, and coming forward as prisoners."

The Americans rejoiced. Out on the field, bodies lay everywhere. There were well over two thousand British killed or wounded. The Americans had as little as twenty killed and wounded. The battle had destroyed the final hopes of the British in America. And in a cruel twist of fate, it was learned later that a peace treaty had been signed on December 24, 1814. But word had not reached New Orleans in time.

The battle of New Orleans made Andrew Jackson a national hero overnight. It was also the final revenge for the cut he had received from the British officer as a fourteen-year-old. He had lived from that day to see a whole British army destroyed. Now he had led the attack himself.

But his powerful victory marked the end of a war that achieved very little. The Americans hoped to capture part or all of Canada. They failed. The British hoped to regain some territory lost in the Revolution. They failed. The capitol had been burned and the country was in ruins.

If ever America needed a hero, it was now. And there was just one man who qualified. Old Hickory. Andrew Jackson had won the biggest land battle of the war. His victory had turned the whole war into a victory.

Shortly after the peace treaty was announced, Rachel joined the general in New Orleans. She hadn't seen him in seven months. Mrs. Jackson was forty-seven and had grown stout over the years. But she still had jet black hair and dancing dark eyes. Her warm smile showed beautiful, almost perfect teeth. And her skin was tanned by the wind and sun of the Hermitage.

Rachel's trip to New Orleans was her first visit to a city larger than Nashville. Her reunion with her husband was a happy one. They were still there on March 15, when the general celebrated his forty-eighth birthday.

Andrew was in a mellow mood, happy for his success in battle. He told the few friends who brought him birthday greetings that his "first wish had been to be useful to my country." But he also spoke of those who were not there, especially his mother.

"How I wish she could have lived to see this day," he said. Then he repeated some of the advice she gave him the last time he saw her. He said she told him to make friends by being honest, keep them by being steadfast; to be truthful, sincere, and brave.

"Gentlemen," said Andrew Jackson. "Those words have been the law of my life."

For Rachel Jackson, it seemed time for a change. Andrew had been away from home so much, either on business or at war. Now, at long last, perhaps she would have a quiet life with her husband at her side. The money he had made as a general got them out of debt for the first time since 1796. Perhaps it was time for a new beginning.

The Jacksons returned to the Hermitage in May. The people in Nashville greeted him the same way others had, like a hero. They lined the trail as he made the final leg of the journey by horseback for all to see him. But as soon as he reached the Hermitage Andrew collapsed. He had willed himself to stay well just long enough to complete his task.

For nearly five months Rachel nursed her husband. Sometimes she sat by his bedside and fed him like a child. But Andrew loved the attention, especially after the hardships of battle and the loneliness of being far from home.

His strength returned as well as his fortunes. The country's economy was getting stronger. By October of 1815, the Jacksons had more than twenty-two thousand dollars in the Nashville Bank.

It was during Jackson's trip to Washington in the fall that someone first suggested he run for president. Politicians noted for the first time that this Indian fighter and winning general was not just a rugged, uncouth frontiersman. Andrew carried himself with dignity and poise. His tall, straight frame and magnificent head of gray hair already gave him the look of a respected senior politician.

Back home at the Hermitage, Jackson continued to attend to business and enjoy the company of his family. Time passed. Maybe, just maybe, Rachel hoped, this time he'll stay. Then in the late summer of 1817, he left the Hermitage to visit a dying friend, John Hutchings, who was living near Huntsville.

Hutchings' wife had died several years earlier, and the dying man's final wish was for Andrew to take his six-year-old son. With a tear in his eye for his old friend, Jackson agreed. Another boy joined the Hermitage family, to grow up with Andrew, Jr., and Lincoyer, the young Creek Indian boy.

While he was with John Hutchings, he received an order from the new president, James Monroe. The president wanted General Jackson to lead federal troops to the border of Georgia and Florida. Seminole Indians were causing some problems there. Florida was still under Spanish rule as well.

"They want me to pursue the enemy where necessary, but not to attack a Spanish Fort," Jackson said to an aide. Then he asked the next question: "What do they really want?"

He wrote to Monroe: "Let it be known to me

through any channel that the possession of the Floridas would be desirable and in sixty days it will be accomplished."

Jackson always claimed that a U.S. representative replied, giving him the president's approval to take control of Florida. The letter, Jackson said, told him to do his job and then let the politicians pick up the pieces. President Monroe later said he had not given the approval.

But Jackson went ahead. He started by capturing several Indian villages and a Spanish fort at St. Mark. He had two British subjects he thought were traitors executed as an example. Then he marched on Pensacola. The Spanish quickly fled. As he predicted, there was very little bloodshed. Within five months the hostile Indians were gone and Andrew Jackson had conquered Florida.

On May 13, 1818, the general left for home, once again hailed a hero by the people. The settlers near the Florida border looked upon him as a savior. Their lives and lands were now much safer. Some saw new lands opening to them in Florida. Still others saw Andrew Jackson as a man who got things done. His victories were victories for the American people.

But there was a political storm over his actions. Spain wanted its land back and Jackson punished. At first, President Monroe's administration was against Jackson. Only John Quincy Adams, the secretary of state, stood up for him. As for the general, he refused to budge. He stood by what he did, and took complete responsibility for it.

"I have never shrunk from my responsibility and never will," he said.

Nor would he say he misunderstood his orders. Some members of Congress criticized him. But even his enemies and those who thought him wrong knew one thing. The people loved him. He was their hero. There was no way the country or government could punish Andrew Jackson.

Within sixty days, everything changed. The administration praised his campaign. Any moves to punish him were dropped. On February 22, 1819, Spain turned Florida over to the United States. It was another complete victory for Andrew Jackson.

He left Washington listening to the wild cheers of the people. More than ever, he seemed to be a man for his time, a man whose strength fit the mood of a growing nation.

So he headed home once more. But for how long? Now even Andrew Jackson wasn't sure. Shortly after he reached the Hermitage and greeted everyone, he called Rachel out into the garden.

"Mrs. Jackson," he said. "I would truly love to build you a new house."

# CHAPTER ELEVEN

# Private Life, But Not For Long

Perhaps it was because he was away so often that Andrew wanted to do something special for Rachel. A new home, to replace the old log blockhouse, seemed the perfect answer. He also may have looked upon it as a parting gift to her. Weakened by illnesses, he wasn't sure how much time he had left. In fact, when a neighbor, William B. Lewis, saw the site for the new house, he suggested another location to the general.

"No, sir," Jackson answered. "Mrs. Jackson chose this spot, and she shall have her wish. I am going to build this house for her. I don't expect to live in it myself."

The new house was built in a private meadow. Much of the bricks and the oak timbers were prepared right at the plantation. The front of the home would be about eighty-five feet across.

The Jacksons planned a small porch in the front, more like a New England home than a Southern plantation. There was a main hall that ran the entire length of the house. On both sides of the hall were parlors. Behind the parlor on the left was the dining room, and behind the one on the right was the main bedroom, where Rachel and Andrew would sleep.

A staircase led to the second floor where there were five or six sleeping rooms. General Jackson's office was a small brick building on the west side of the house. Both the kitchen and servant's quarters were in the rear. It wasn't a huge house, but it was the mark of a wealthy man.

"You furnish the house any way you wish," Andrew told Rachel. "I can have anything you want sent here."

So she did. The house was built and the new furnishings began arriving. Family possessions were moved from the old blockhouse. Andrew also hired a gardener to lay out the grounds.

The new house would have a beautiful lawn shaded by large trees. From her bedroom window, Rachel would look upon an acre of neatly arranged flowers and a series of curving, brick-edged walkways. It was quite a lovely site.

The new Hermitage was completed in the spring of 1819. That summer, the Jacksons hosted a very important visitor there. President James Monroe decided to tour that part of the country. When he passed through Tennessee he stopped at the home of Andrew Jackson.

The president asked the nation's most popular general to accompany him through parts of Tennessee and into Georgia. Suddenly, the crowds were larger, the applause louder, the cheers and cries stronger. Through Knoxville and over the Cumberland Road to Nashville, the applause never stopped.

And it didn't take a brilliant politician to figure out why the tour had picked up.

"It ain't the president we come to see," said one frontiersman, still wearing his buckskin shirt and pants, and carrying his rifle. "It's the general. Ain't none better 'n Andy Jackson."

Of course, the general had not meant to upstage the president. He soon left the tour and returned to the Hermitage. As much as he enjoyed the people's reaction to him, political office was not part of his immediate plans.

The next two years were difficult for Andrew. He felt restless. He wrote President Monroe saying he was ready to resign from the army if his country no longer needed him. The letter began: "I am wearied with public life . . ."

But his country did need him. First it was thought the army might be needed again in Florida. Spain had gone back on some of her promises. But in the spring of 1821, the problems were settled. President Monroe asked Andrew to become the first governor of Florida. It was a job he didn't really want, but Old Hickory felt he had to accept.

He and Mrs. Jackson traveled back to New Orleans by steamboat; the journey took eight days. They even brought their own coach with them. It had new glass in all the windows. There were lace curtains over the windows, and the seats had been redone in fine leather. They would use it to travel from New Orleans to Pensacola, Florida.

Though they arrived in style, Andrew found the job of governor dull. He had finally resigned from the army and that depressed him even more. He also hated the hot, muggy weather in Florida, and the huge mosquitoes that seemed to be everywhere. On October 5, 1821, he resigned his office as governor.

"Having organized the government and it being in full operation," he wrote, "I'm going home."

And home he went. With his carriage drawn by four white horses, he left Pensacola for good, his smiling wife at his side. This time, he truly planned to spend the rest of his days at the Hermitage.

Andrew and Rachel stopped in New Orleans and bought more things for their new house. There were seven cases of furniture and a set of new silverware for their table. They had bought a magnificent mahogany wood bed with hand-carved trim. There was a new sideboard for their china dishes and various whiskeys and tobaccos.

When they arrived home, the Hermitage quickly sprung to life. Fires burned brightly in every room and old friends dropped by to greet the popular couple. Perhaps this time Andrew would stay. He was nearly fifty-five years old and at times looked ten years older. His life had been far from easy. It had, indeed, robbed him of a good deal of his health.

As for Rachel, she had heard her husband vow to remain at home before. This time she felt he meant it. But she knew if his country needed his services, he'd go.

In a letter to her niece, Mary Donelson, she expressed her greatest fear:

"I do hope they will now leave Mr. Jackson alone. He is not a well man and never will be unless they allow him to rest. He has done his share for the country. In the thirty years of our wedded life he has not spent one-fourth of his days under his own roof."

Rachel was writing her niece because she had a new worry. With the election of 1824 approaching, there was more and more talk about Andrew Jackson running for president of the United States.

Andrew was never out of touch with the political issues in the country. He subscribed to some twenty newspapers from different parts of the land, and read each one cover to cover. They were always strewn about his office. A number of his friends were either in politics or interested observers. The U.S. senator from Tennessee, John Henry Eaton, often came to visit. He would tell the general about the happenings in Washington and in Congress.

But it was one thing to follow politics and another to be thought of as president. Yet changes in the country caused many people to look for a new kind of president.

The first two presidents, George Washington and John Adams, were Federalists. They based the presidency on what the founding fathers had put in the Constitution, having one government rule the union of states. Yet some began to feel there was too much power in the federal capitol, and not enough with the individual states.

Thomas Jefferson, the third president, was a member

of the Republican Party. His party saw the country as a republic, a union of many states, with states represented in federal government. Jefferson served two terms, and was followed by James Madison and then James Monroe. They were Republicans also. The old Federalist Party of Washington and Adams died out more or less.

But there was still grumbling. For one thing, all of the presidents, except Adams, were born in Virginia. Some began to call them the "royal family." Many people still felt that the government should be run by people of wealth, people from the right families.

But the United States was growing rapidly. There were many different kinds of people. Government by a "royal" few was exactly what the colonists had fought to get free of in 1776. During Monroe's second term, which began in early 1821, there was more talk than ever about changing the way things were done.

Complaints about all the presidents coming from one state continued. One wealthy Virginia politician seemed to follow another right to the White House. Instead of a central group nominating the next president, why shouldn't the state governments nominate candidates? That way, it would be more of a real election.

Andrew Jackson and his good friends often talked about these questions. On more than one occasion either John Overton, John Eaton, or William Lewis suggested that Andrew would make a good candidate for president. At first, he just laughed at their suggestions. It was during one of these sessions when he said:

"I know what I am fit for. I can command a body of men in a rough way, but I am not fit to be president."

Later, when the talk began to spread, he continued to offer up reasons why it shouldn't be. Simply put, he didn't want it.

"I have no desire," he said, "nor do I expect ever to be called to fill the presidential chair, but should this be the case, it shall be without exertion on my part."

As for Mrs. Jackson, the talk struck fear in her heart. All she ever wanted was privacy and her husband. Now there was talk of the highest office in the land.

"They talk of his being president," she said. "In this as all else I can say only, the Lord's will be done. But I hope he may not be called again to the strife and empty honors of public place."

Most people thought the president named in 1824 would be one of three of James Monroe's cabinet members. They were John Quincy Adams, son of the second president, William Crawford, and Henry Clay. But there was a movement growing in the state of Tennessee. A strong editorial in two of the state's newspapers said, in part:

"The name of Andrew Jackson to a document would command more respect than the signatures of all the cabinet members in the nation."

Another story in the *Nashville Clarion* said that for "having done more than any man now living, General Jackson was unquestionably the choice of the people."

Jackson continued to deny any interest in the job. In

fact, he kept offering reasons why he shouldn't be president.

"I am no longer a young man," he told a friend. "I can't stand the fatigues and stresses I used to. And my health isn't good. Each time I become sick I mend more slowly."

Yet in July of 1822, the Tennessee legislature met and nominated Andrew Jackson for president of the United States. It was the first time in the history of the United States that one of the individual states had nominated a candidate for president.

The general took the news calmly. He was flattered, but he didn't think the nomination would go too far. That didn't stop the word from spreading. Posters reading: "Old Hickory, the Nation's Hero and the People's Friend," began appearing everywhere.

Another favorite of Jackson supporters was to simply holler, "JANUARY 8, 1815" or "BATTLE OF NEW ORLEANS!" Everyone knew what that meant.

The next step was to get Andrew back in the spotlight. That happened in October of 1823, when the general was once again elected to the Senate.

"I have been elected senator," he wrote John Coffee, "a circumstance which I regret more than any other in my life. To leave Mrs. Jackson fills me, as well as her, with much regret."

Once again, he answered the call to duty. As was his custom, he rode to Washington on horseback. He traveled the eight hundred and sixty miles with only John Henry Eaton and a servant.

133

In Washington, he began acting more like a politician. First, he ended his long-standing feud with Thomas Hart Benton, now a senator. Then he held a dinner and invited his three competitors for the presidency—Crawford, Clay, and Adams. Shortly afterward, John Eaton wrote a letter to Rachel, stating in part:

"It will afford you great pleasure to know that all his old quarrels have been settled. The general is in harmony and good understanding with everybody."

People in Washington were getting to know Jackson, and they were liking what they found. Representative Daniel Webster, a polite New Englander not used to frontier people, wrote his brother, saying: "General Jackson's manners are more presidential than those of any of the candidates. He is grave, mild, and reserved. My wife is decidedly for him."

And Senator Elijah Hunt Mills of Massachusetts, a man who had violently opposed Jackson when the general invaded Florida, also had a change of heart. During the Florida campaign, Mills had called Jackson "little advanced in civilization over the Indians with whom he made war."

Now Mills told his wife that "those opinions were unfounded. He is exactly the man with whom you would be delighted."

So Andrew Jackson was no longer just an uncouth frontiersman. Nor was he simply a ferocious soldier. The charm that young girls had seen in Salisbury years before always remained. Despite his various ills, he still cut a bold figure. The sheer force of his personality could be overwhelming.

The campaign of 1824 continued. By early fall, the polls showed Jackson leading the field and gaining. Would he indeed be the next president? Time would tell. Despite his popularity, he still had regrets. He expressed them in a letter to John Coffee.

"How much your situation is to be envied," Jackson wrote, "and how prudent you have been to keep yourself free of political life, surrounded as you are by your lovely children, and amiable wife; you ought not to abandon it for anything on earth."

Finally, the election came. When the results were in, Andrew Jackson had received 152,901 votes to John Quincy Adams' 114,023. That gave Old Hickory 99 electoral votes, Adams 84, Crawford 41, and Clay 27. But Jackson had not won a majority of the electoral votes. By the laws of the Constitution, the election would have to be decided by a House of Representatives' vote.

Now there was the threat of a deal. Many predicted that Henry Clay held the crucial cards.

"You watch," said one Jackson supporter. "Clay will throw his votes to Adams in return for a cabinet post."

"But if that happens, the man with the most popular votes won't win. The general's supporters won't stand for that."

"They'll have to, at least for another four years."

And that's just what happened. Clay threw his support to Adams, giving the Massachusetts native enough votes to become the nation's sixth president. Three days after Adams was sworn in, he named Henry Clay Secretary of State.

Andrew Jackson accepted his narrow defeat with dignity and grace. When he met John Quincy Adams after the election was over he simply bowed and wished Mr. Adams well. He once again resigned from the Senate and returned to his home.

But it didn't take long for the cards to go right back on the table. In the fall of 1825, the Tennessee legislature immediately placed the general's name in nomination for the presidency. The next election was still three years away.

# CHAPTER TWELVE

# Triumph and Tragedy

The three years passed swiftly. Senator Eaton wrote Jackson every few days. It wasn't long before he set their basic campaign strategy. He said:

"All that is necessary for you is to be still and quiet. This administration, wretched and rotten, is already crumbling."

Perhaps, in part, because of the way the election was decided, John Quincy Adams had a difficult time as president. The party was hopelessly split between Jackson men and Adams men.

A master politician from New York, Martin Van Buren, a former Adams supporter, came to the Hermitage. He offered his full services to Andrew Jackson. Van Buren would prove a valuable friend.

By this time, Jackson's enemies knew he would be tough to stop. They looked for ways to criticize him. Once again they began to talk about Lewis Robards, Rachel, and Andrew. Stories of the two weddings reappeared in many newspapers. Some papers in the East began calling Rachel a bigamist, a woman with two husbands. The general was called a liar and a wife stealer.

More than once, the general began cleaning his dueling pistols. But his friends stopped him. A presidential candidate simply could not go out and fight a duel. All he could do was struggle to hold his temper while his friends and political allies defended both him and Rachel.

Besides the political mudslinging, one other sad event clouded the pre-election period. In 1827, Lincoyer died of tuberculosis. The young Creek Indian boy had grown tall and handsome. He was a popular figure at the Hermitage, and a good friend to Andrew, Jr., and the other young people. He was buried in the garden, like all members of the family.

The Jacksons' attention turned back to the election. President John Quincy Adams was trying to win a second term. But against Andrew Jackson and the hundreds of new voters in the South and West, he had no chance. The 1828 election was a landslide.

Though the eastern states still voted for Adams, Andrew Jackson won the popular vote, 647,276 to 508,064. The electoral vote was even more lopsided. Old Hickory had 178 electoral votes to just 83 for John Quincy Adams. Andrew Jackson had been elected the seventh President of the United States.

Upon hearing the results, Andrew Jackson sat down and wrote his friend, John Coffee. "I am filled with gratitude. Still, my mind is depressed."

The depression was for Rachel. He knew how hard

*Andrew Jackson was elected seventh president of the United States.*

the election had been for her, and that all but took away
the joy of winning the office. Rachel herself admitted:

"For Mr. Jackson's sake I am glad. For my own part,
I never wished it."

Once the election was over, Rachel Jackson's health
began to fail. All the courage she had needed during the
election seemed to drain out of her all at once. She grew
sad and tired. One friend noted:

"From the moment the election was over, her energy
subsided, her spirits drooped, and her health declined."

139

A young lawyer and friend, Henry R. Wise, called at the Hermitage. He noted that "Mrs. Jackson talked low but quick, with a short and wheezing breath."

Now plans had to be made for the inauguration, when Jackson would be sworn in as president. There was a great banquet planned in Nashville on December 23, the anniversary of the first night of his battle at New Orleans. Yet the general thought about none of this. All his thoughts were on his wife. Everyone was worried about her. She was under a doctor's care and her mental state was not good. She spoke very little.

On December 17, she suffered what must have been a major heart attack. There were no wonder drugs back then, no operations that could save lives. The doctors did what they could. With Andrew at her side throughout the night, Rachel seemed to sleep peacefully. In the morning, some of her strength returned.

During the next few days, husband and wife sat by the fire. Rachel seemed more cheerful than she had been in a while. The general never left his wife alone. She must have wished it had always been like that. But on Sunday night, December 22, Rachel insisted Andrew get some sleep.

"Please, Mr. Jackson. You must rest. They'll be expecting you at the banquet tomorrow."

"I'll not leave you," he said quietly.

"For awhile, just to go to the banquet. You can't let all those people down. I'll be here when you return."

Andrew finally went to bed. Then sometime during

the night, Rachel's longtime maid, Hannah, heard her cry out: "I am fainting!"

Rachel collapsed in Hannah's arms as Andrew burst into the room. The two put Rachel into the bed and called for the doctor. This time it was too late. She was gone.

Andrew Jackson immediately went into deep mourning. He refused to leave his wife's side. Only when she was being dressed for burial did he consent to leave the room. Toward evening, someone convinced him to sip a little coffee. He ate and drank nothing else all day.

At one o'clock in the afternoon of December 24, 1828, Rachel Jackson was buried in the garden, just one hundred and fifty paces from the east door of the main house. Nearly ten thousand people, twice the population of Nashville, came to the Hermitage for the funeral.

The roads were choked with horses, buggies, carriages, and wagons of every kind. No one was turned away. There were rich and poor, white and black. Certainly her husband was the famous one; but Rachel Jackson had been kind and patient. She was loved and admired by many as a good person, a good wife, a good mother, a good friend.

Once the funeral was over, people began asking the obvious question. What of the general? He wasn't in good health to begin with. Would he now fail? Or would he decide that without Rachel he wasn't up to being president of the United States? These were hard questions. He had openly shed tears at her graveside, later saying:

"I know 'tis unmanly, but these tears are due her virtues. She has shed many for me."

141

*On December 24, 1828 Rachel Jackson was buried in the garden.*

On January 18, 1829, the general stepped aboard a steamboat at Nashville to begin the trip to Washington. He was still in deep mourning.

"My heart is nearly broke," he said. "I try to summon up my usual fortitude, but in vain."

Word spread quickly that the general was coming. What kind of a president would he make? After all, he was not one of the Virginia politicians. He was not formally educated. Many considered him violent and unmannered, a product of the frontier.

Yet he was very popular with the people. In fact,

more than anyone who came before him, Andrew Jackson was a president for all the people. Many more welcomed him than feared him. Yet it was the fear of the unknown that had some politicians worried.

Daniel Webster, who had liked Jackson when he first met him a few years earlier, said this about the general's arrival:

"Nobody knows what he will do when he does come. My opinion is that when he comes he will bring a breeze with him. Which way it will blow, I cannot tell. My fear is stronger than my hope."

Despite rumors about the general's failing health, men and women flocked to Washington for the inauguration. It was a crowd never before seen in the nation's capitol. Tennessee backwoodsmen and frontiersmen from the Northwest mixed with Irish immigrants from the East.

"I never saw anything like it before," Daniel Webster said. "They really seem to think the country is to be rescued from some dreadful danger."

In early 1829, Pennsylvania Avenue was the main road past the White House, though it was still unpaved. It connected the President's home with the Capitol Building, which was still being rebuilt after the British burned it in 1814. In addition, there were four smaller brick buildings, one each for the Departments of State, Treasury, War, and Navy.

But to the north and south there were just scattered

houses and farms. To go from one to another, a traveler would have to fight his way through swamps, across ditches, or over hills thick with pine trees.

On March 4, 1829, Supreme Court Chief Justice John Marshall read the oath of office to Andrew Jackson. The new president was nearly sixty-two years old, but to many he looked much older. Yet he stood straight, and when he spoke his voice was steady. He could feel the ivory miniature hanging around his neck. On it was a small portrait of his wife Rachel. He wore it everywhere. It made him feel that she was with him, still close to him.

After his inauguration speech, which few heard above the noise of the crowd, the celebration began. The president rode a horse slowly to the White House as the crowds surged on all sides. His friends had to lock arms to get him safely inside. But even the White House was mobbed with people. Almost as soon as he arrived, he had to be taken out the back door. Back at his hotel, Andrew Jackson, president of the United States, collapsed in exhaustion.

# CHAPTER THIRTEEN

# Mr. President

No one knew just what kind of a president Andrew Jackson would make. Old Hickory himself probably didn't know. All his life he had hated administrative work. He just didn't like sitting behind a desk pushing papers.

But Andrew Jackson always had a strong sense of duty to his country. Now his duty was to serve the highest office in the land. And that was why he came to Washington, determined to do the best job he could. It was his duty!

The new job took some getting used to, especially so soon after the death of his wife. When he took office, Jackson's friends said he looked grief-stricken and weary. He had a hacking cough which often made his whole body shake. He also suffered from frequent headaches. Some thought they were caused by years of chewing tobacco, a frontier habit he brought right into the White House.

Yet he still had an iron will that kept him going. He surrounded himself with trusted friends. His nephew, Jack Donelson, was a valuable White House aide. Donelson's wife, Emily, served as White House hostess, the job that would have been Rachel's.

The president didn't really like or trust his vice-president, John C. Calhoun of South Carolina. Instead, he leaned to Secretary of State Martin Van Buren as his most trusted political ally. Though they were complete opposites in many ways, Van Buren respected and admired Jackson. He told friends there was "something in that noble old man" that moved him.

Old friends like John Overton and John Coffee were available whenever needed. William Lewis accepted a minor post just to stay in Washington and be near the President. Other young men such as Amos Kendall, Isaac Hill, and Francis Blair had impressed the president with their writing and editing skills. He gave them government posts.

They helped produce an administration newspaper called *The Globe*, which promoted the president's causes. Because they were unofficial advisors, they became known as the "Kitchen Cabinet." They were consulted as much or more often than the official cabinet.

Slowly, the Jackson style began to show. While there would always be enemies, he began to impress more and more people. Said Martin Van Buren:

"I never knew a man more free from conceit or one to whom it was a pleasure to listen patiently to what might be said by him upon any subject."

"The character of his mind," said Thomas Hart Benton, "was that of judgement, with a rapid and almost intuitive perception, followed by an instant and decisive action."

Another congressman, Louis McLane of Delaware,

said that "General Jackson was one of the most rapid reasoners I have ever met with. He jumps to a conclusion before I can start my premises."

Still another observer saw his mind this way. "To him, knowledge seemed unnecessary. He saw intuitively into everything and reached a conclusion by a shortcut while others were beating the bush for the game."

It was the same way he had conducted his battles. He reacted quickly to the situation and made a decision. Just as he would consult his military aides, he would discuss problems with his cabinet. But when the moment for action came, he always made up his own mind.

There were certainly some sticky issues in his first term. One of them had absolutely nothing to do with national or world affairs. The president's friend and secretary of war, John Eaton, had married the daughter of an innkeeper. Many of the Washington wives, including Emily Donelson, felt Peggy Eaton wasn't worthy of them. She came from a low background and was said to be a loose woman.

When the others refused to accept her, Andrew Jackson exploded. To him, it was almost like Rachel being criticized all over again. He ordered the others to accept her. But the problem just wouldn't go away. At one point, an angry Jackson even said:

"I would resign the presidency sooner than desert my friend Eaton."

It finally took drastic steps, suggested by Martin Van Buren, to settle the dispute. All the cabinet members resigned and were given new jobs. The president gave John

Eaton a new job outside of Washington. It was a needless, time-consuming problem. But it showed how loyal a friend Andrew Jackson could be.

There were continued problems with the Indians. As always, the dispute was over land that the white man wanted. John Quincy Adams had been kind to the Indians, very kind. But Andrew Jackson's position may have been more realistic.

The president knew about white and Indian clashes firsthand. His experience went all the way back to the Waxhaws. Perhaps it was wrong to push these native American Indians off land they had lived on for hundreds of years. But Andrew Jackson truly felt that moving the Indians westward was the only way to save them from extinction.

He knew that white men would continue to take over more of the country. At one point, he helped Georgia push peaceful Creeks and Cherokees off of lands the government had once given them. Was it wrong? Perhaps. But Andrew Jackson saw it as the only way. In his farewell address, in 1837, he said this about the Indians:

"The states which had so long been retarded in their improvement by the Indian tribes residing in their midst are at length relieved, and this unhappy race—the original dwellers in our land—are now placed in a situation where we may well hope that they will share in the blessings of civilization."

Again, he felt he had done the right thing.

Another battle the president fought had to do with taxes. The state of South Carolina threatened to undo a federal act of 1828. The act required them to pay taxes on imported goods. South Carolina wanted to break the law and not pay the taxes.

New England, with its many factories, favored the high tax. It made foreign goods expensive. People would buy New England goods instead. The Southern states, which normally imported more goods in exchange for its cotton, wanted a low tax. Now South Carolina threatened to ignore the law.

There was more to it than that. It became a matter of states rights versus the federal union. Who had the power to make laws, an individual state, like South Carolina, or the union of all the states? How would the president react to South Carolina's threats? After all, Andrew Jackson was a Southerner. He would understand.

On April 13, 1830, there was a dinner party given in memory of Thomas Jefferson. President Jackson was to give a toast that night. What he said would show which side he took on the issue.

When it came time, everyone was quiet. President Jackson stood and raised his glass.

"Our Union," he said. "It must be preserved!"

Jackson had decided that the needs of the Federal government were more important than one state's needs.

Vice President Calhoun, from South Carolina, then rose. It was his turn.

"The Union," he said, glass raised. "Next to our liberty, most dear."

Calhoun was clearly stating that states' freedom was

more important than the Union. That was the final break between two men who never really liked each other.

The debates grew hotter and hotter. Finally, South Carolina threatened to secede from the Union. The battle continued right into 1833. Then Andrew Jackson got tough. South Carolina found it was threatening the wrong man:

"If one drop of blood be shed in defiance of the laws of the United States," declared the president, "I will hang the first man of them I can get my hands on to the first tree I can find."

Thomas Hart Benton, a friend who used to be an enemy, knew the president wasn't kidding. Said Senator Benton:

"If Andrew Jackson starts talking about hanging people, you better go out and find some rope."

And later, when the talk of not paying the taxes continued, the old general acted again. "If the South Carolina Assembly authorizes twelve thousand men to resist the law, I will order thirty thousand to execute it."

The final showdown came early in 1833. Would South Carolina resist? Andrew Jackson made sure it would not. He had thirty-five thousand troops ready to march at a moment's notice. His only words:

"Our Union will be preserved."

His friend, Martin Van Buren, later said that Old Hickory "yearned to lead this force in person."

As always, the general was ready to lead his troops.

Finally, on March 15, 1833, South Carolina gave up the struggle. The taxes would be paid. Fear of civil war was gone. And on his sixty-sixth birthday, Andrew Jackson's popularity was greater than any president's had ever been.

It has been said that Andrew Jackson was not a deep thinker, especially when compared to some other presidents like Thomas Jefferson and John Adams. Yet he saw this states' rights struggle as the beginning of something more than a protest over a tax. It was a clash between North and South, and it would one day erupt into the most terrible war in our history. The real issue was slavery. Jackson said it a short time later, after South Carolina's fight had ended:

"The South intends to blow up a storm on the slave question. This ought to be met, for be assured these men would do any act to destroy this Union and form a southern confederacy."

Andrew Jackson was a slave owner all his life. It was something he had grown up with in the South. It was the way of life. He treated the black slaves at the Hermitage fairly and decently. Yet he saw a violent, North-South storm over slavery coming. He didn't say whether slavery was right or wrong, only that it was a threat to the Union.

In the end, he was right. Less than thirty years later, South Carolina would lead the Southern states out of the Union. The great Civil War would divide the nation in blood. One can only wonder if that war would have taken place with Andrew Jackson in the White House. For when that conflict did erupt some twenty-five years later, someone cried out:

"Oh, for an hour of old Andrew Jackson."

That was probably the most explosive issue of Jackson's presidency. It was perhaps his greatest victory. But there were difficult times as well. The president's health was not good. He tired easily and had a number of medical emergencies.

In January of 1832, a doctor removed the Benton bullet from his left arm. Old Hickory just grasped his walking stick hard and grimaced with pain as the doctor cut the bullet free. That night, he went to a dinner party. Soon his arm felt much better.

But the other bullet near his heart could never be touched. And it continued to cause him lung problems. From time to time he wrote people to tell them he wished he was back home. He was again tired of public life. And he never stopped mourning for Rachel.

Every night, after he got ready for bed, the president would remove the ivory miniature from around his neck. He would then prop it up on the bedside table. Mrs. Jackson's picture was the last thing he saw at night and the first thing his eyes saw in the morning. Then he would read from Rachel's Bible until he fell asleep.

The President was overjoyed when his son, Andrew, Jr., married a fine young girl named Sarah Yorke. Old Hickory loved her like a daughter. She was the only one permitted to read from Rachel's Bible to him. Finally, he sent young Andrew and Sarah home to run the Hermitage for him. Soon after, in one of his letters, he wrote:

"My only ambition is to get to the Hermitage so

*Every night he would read from Rachel's Bible until he fell asleep.*

soon as the interest of my country will permit, and there to put my house in order and go to sleep alongside my dear departed wife."

The old man was getting tired.

Yet in the autumn of 1832, he was elected, by a landslide, to a second term. He defeated old rival Henry Clay. This time Martin Van Buren was Jackson's vice president. And in some ways, his second term in office would be harder than the first.

He would fight a long, slow battle against the United States Bank. It was a private bank set up to keep public money for twenty years. The bank was established in 1816. The President wanted the arrangement to end, for good, in 1836. He felt the bank was too powerful and

153

could hurt the country. Smaller state banks would be safer, he felt.

The battle against the Bank and its president, Nicholas Biddle, was a difficult one. But in the end, Old Hickory won.

It was amazing that Andrew still had the energy for these drawn-out political battles. The years were passing and old age was closing in. It was also catching up with his friends. In 1833, he lost both John Overton and John Coffee. Both men had been loyal and close to the President for many years.

"The world is emptying of familiar faces," the president wrote, sadly.

He tried to keep many young people around him at the White House. The Donelsons and their friends were big favorites. They brought life and energy to a world full of politics.

In the summer of 1833, he took a vacation trip. He started at Fredericksburg, Virginia, where he took part in a ceremony. At one point, a young man approached him as if to greet him. Suddenly, he punched the president in the face.

Aides grabbed at the man, who broke loose and ran through a door. Now the president was running after him, his cane raised. Someone identified the man as Robert B. Randolph, a former Navy officer. He was later captured, though the president refused to press charges. But he told people privately that if he had been on his feet and ready, Randolph "never would have moved with life from the tracks he stood in."

Even at his age, Andrew Jackson was ready for action and willing to fight. That never changed. But later in the same trip, his lung began to bleed again, and he finally collapsed.

One of Jackson's final questions as president was the war in Texas. The Texans, led by an old friend, Sam Houston, were fighting for their independence from Mexico. Many wanted him to name Texas a state, but the president hesitated. He knew it would open the slavery question again and anger the North. To those who never believed it, he was a smart politician. Texas was later granted statehood, in 1845.

In 1834, the Hermitage was having money troubles. Andrew, Jr., was not a shrewd businessman. In October of that year, the Hermitage was swept by a fire. No one was hurt, but the house was heavily damaged. It would have to be rebuilt.

By the summer of 1836, the new Hermitage was completed. It was a beautiful southern-style home with large white columns in front. There were still money problems, as another cotton crop failed. Andrew could not wait to get home and take over once again.

In November of 1836, his second term ended. Martin Van Buren was elected to be the next president. Shortly afterward, Andrew's lung began to bleed again. It almost killed him. But once again he amazed everyone with his recovery.

One who did not recover was Emily Donelson. The president's niece had been ill. She suddenly took a turn

*The new Hermitage was a beautiful southern-style home with large white columns in front.*

for the worse. On December 20, she died at the age of twenty-eight at home in Tennessee. Her husband was still two days away when she died.

It was another sharp blow for the old general. He had loved his niece and she had served him well as White House hostess. His only comfort was that he was going home soon. His two terms were at an end. History would remember him as a good president, a man who protected the country well.

Whatever his critics said, Andrew Jackson was one of the most popular presidents ever.

At Van Buren's inauguration, all eyes were on the outgoing President. As Thomas Hart Benton wrote, "For once, the rising was eclipsed by the setting sun."

When Andrew Jackson walked down the Capitol

steps for the final time Thomas Hart Benton recalled that a mighty shout burst from the crowd.

"It was the kind of cry such as power never commanded, nor man in power received. It was affection, gratitude and admiration. I felt an emotion which had never passed through me before."

Unlike many presidents, Andrew Jackson left the White House more popular than ever. He was loved, respected, and admired.

He came to Washington without personal goals. Very few presidents can make that claim. In fact, he came as a man saddened and broken over the death of his wife. Yet despite his grief and poor health, he was the strongest president since George Washington, the most powerful president until Abraham Lincoln. No one dared cross paths with Old Hickory.

At home again, he was happy to be with friends and family.

"I am very thankful to a kind providence for sparing me to reach my home," he wrote. "I hope rest in due time may restore my health so as to be enabled to amuse myself in riding over my farm and visiting my neighbors."

Good health was not always there. His retirement years were marked by periods of illness and pain. Yet there were also good times. People came from far and wide to visit him. At home in the Hermitage, he didn't mind. He was close to Rachel and surrounded by family.

There was always a battle with debts. The general had to sell land and horses to pay debts. In 1840, he jour-

*Andrew Jackson left the White House as a loved and respected figure.*

neyed to New Orleans to celebrate the twenty-fifth anniversary of his famous battle. He was weak and ill. He would not have gone, but it was still a chance to raise money to pay his son's debts.

There were times when those around him wondered

how long he could survive. In April of 1842, he told his friend Frank Blair: "I have been scarcely able to write—with pain in my ears, head and eyes, it is quite an effort."

Blair's answer to him was, "Your life is of the soul, more than the body."

In a way it was true. He had a strength of spirit that was second to none. And he was still called upon to help. In late 1843 and early 1844, President John Tyler asked Old Hickory to help get Texas out of Mexico's grasp for good. Jackson wrote letters to Texas president Sam Houston and other politicians to help get the job done.

By early 1845, the end was near. The general was getting weaker. He was blind in one eye and had trouble hearing. His nights were spent propped up in bed. During the day, he rested in a pillowed chair. Friends came as often as his strength would permit.

In early June more bleeding in his lung made him even weaker. His last letter was written on June 6, to James Polk, the new president of the United States. People were now coming to the Hermitage for the final visit. Old friends, neighbors, whites and blacks came. There was sadness everywhere.

Though dying, Old Hickory was in control to the end. William Lewis came to see him at noon.

He calmly gave Lewis his last messages for Sam Houston, Thomas Hart Benton, and Frank Blair.

He was able to say goodbye to every member of the family and all the household servants, kissing and blessing each one of them. The one he held the longest was his little granddaughter, named Rachel Jackson.

"My dear children, and friends, and servants," he said. "I hope and trust to meet you all in Heaven, both white and black."

At five-thirty, Andrew, Jr., asked his father if he still knew who he was. The old man answered, "Yes, I know you. I would know you all if I could see."

A half hour later he was gone. A life that had been filled with so much action, from the Revolutionary War to the White House, ended peacefully. The general was seventy-eight years old. And nearly seventeen years after his beloved Rachel had passed away, Andrew Jackson would at last join her once more.

# GLOSSARY

**Backwoodsman**
A frontier man; a person with somewhat rough manners.

**Benton, Thomas Hart**
Senator from Missouri who feuded with Andrew Jackson.

**Blockhouse**
A rough structure of heavy timbers.

**Boston Massacre**
Incident that took place in March, 1770. British soldiers fired on protesting crowds of colonists in Boston, killing five people.

**Boston Tea Party**
In December of 1773, citizens of Boston disguised as Indians secretly boarded British ships and dumped shipments of tea overboard as a protest against taxes.

**Bugle**
A kind of trumpet used for sounding military calls.

**Calhoun, John C.**
A Senator from South Carolina who later became vice-president under Andrew Jackson. He was a strong supporter of states rights.

**Camden**
A town where Andrew Jackson was imprisoned during the American Revolution.

**Cherokee**
Indian Tribe in the Southeastern United States where Andrew Jackson lived.

**Circuit**
A route lawyers and judges would travel along the frontier to towns that had no permanent courts.

**Cockfights**
A country sport in which two gamecocks (roosters) fought until one was killed.

**Concord and Lexington**
Towns in Massachusetts where the first battles of the American Revolution were fought.

**Crawford, Robert**
Andrew Jackson's uncle and the leader of the Waxhaws Militia.

**Creek Indians**
Indian tribe which settled in the Mississippi Territory.

**Crockett, Davy**
Famous frontiersman who fought against the Indians in Andrew Jackson's army.

**Cumberland Valley**
The territory Andrew Jackson lived in and where Nashville was located.

**Declaration of Independence**
Document written by Thomas Jefferson at the 2nd Continental Congress which proclaims America's independence from Great Britain.

**Dragoon**
One member of an English military unit, made up of heavily armed troops on horseback.

**Flatboat**
  A boat with a flat bottom and square ends, used to transport goods.
**Gage, Thomas**
  British general during the Revolutionary War.
**Hermitage**
  Andrew Jackson's farm in Tennessee, which was Jackson's final residence.
**Hunter's Hill**
  Andrew Jackson's home in Tennessee.
**Jackson, Rachel Donelson**
  Andrew Jackson's wife.
**Lexington and Concord**
  Places where the opening battles of the American Revolution occurred.
**Marksmen**
  Men who were good at shooting.
**McNairy, John**
  A judge who was a friend of Andrew Jackson.
**Minutemen**
  Patriotic American colonists who were always prepared to fight the British "in a minute."
**Muskets**
  A large, heavy, long-barrelled firearm, carried on the shoulder.
**Patriots**
  Colonists who fought for independence.
**Red Eagle (William Weatherford)**
  The Creek warrior chief who led his tribe in war against the U.S.
**Sevier, "Nolichucky" Jack**
  Revolutionary War hero in Andrew Jackson's home territory of the Carolinas. He fought like an Indian and he and his men often dressed in buckskin.
**State Constitution**
  The constitution which governs a particular state.
**Tecumseh**
  Great Indian chief who tried to unite the Indian tribes.
**Tennessee State Militia**
  Militia in which Andrew Jackson served as a leader.
**Tomahawk**
  A light ax used by North American Indians as a weapon.
**Tories**
  Colonists loyal to Britain during the American Revolution.
**Wagon Train**
  A line of wagons traveling together across the wilderness.
**Washington, George**
  The general who led the Continental Army against the British during the Revolution, and who later became the first president of the United States.
**Waxhaw Militia Co.**
  Group of patriots who assembled to fight the British in Andrew Jackson's home territory.
**Yorktown**
  Place where the last battle of the war took place, resulting in an American victory.

1. Andrew Jackson was called the first "log cabin" president. What was meant by this?
2. As a young lawyer, Andrew Jackson traveled the "Circuit." Describe what this was.
3. Andrew Jackson grew up in a frontier community called "the Waxhaws." Describe life in a frontier community in Andrew Jackson's time.
4. Andrew Jackson came from the western part of the United States. How were the "West" and "East" of the United States different in Andrew Jackson's time?
5. Andrew Jackson's nickname was "Old Hickory." How did he get this nickname?
6. Briefly describe the Battle of New Orleans. How could this battle have been avoided?
7. Why do you think Andrew Jackson and the Americans won the Battle of New Orleans?
8. What was the public's attitude toward dueling in Andrew Jackson's time? What is the public's attitude today?
9. What was the War of 1812? Name the main cause of the war.
10. Why was Andrew Jackson so popular with the voters of his time? Do you think he would be as popular today?
11. Andrew Jackson's administration is said to have

begun the "spoils system." What does this mean? Do you think the "spoils system" is good or bad? Why?

12. Why was it important for the American troops to gain control of New Orleans during the War of 1812?

13. Research the "Trail of Tears." What does it tell us about the United States during Andrew Jackson's time?

14. Research the Nullification Crisis. What was the crisis about and why was it a threat to the federal government during Andrew Jackson's administration?

15. Research the Indian Removal Act of 1830? What was the justification for taking away the Indian lands? Do you feel the Indians were treated fairly? How should the conflict between the Indians and the white settlers have been solved?

16. Research Andrew Jackson's dispute with the Bank of America. Why did Andrew Jackson oppose the bank?

17. When Andrew Jackson became president, his election was seen as a "triumph of Democracy." Why do you think this was so?

Boardman, Fon W., Jr. *America and the Jacksonian Era, 1825–1850.* H.Z. Walck, 1975.

Dupuy, T.N. *The Military History of Revolutionary War Land Battles.* F. Watts, 1970.

Fleming, Thomas J. "The Battle of Yorktown." *American Heritage, The Magazine of History,* 1968.

Lawson, Don. *The War of 1812, America's Second War for Independence.* Abelard-Shuman, 1966.

Martin, Joseph Plumb. *The Narrative of Some of the Adventures, Dangers and Sufferings of a Revolutionary Soldier.* Arno Press, 1968.

Meltzer, Milton. *Hunted Like a Wolf: The Story of the Seminole War.* Farrar, Straus & Giroux, 1972.

Remini, Robert V. *The Revolutionary Age of Andrew Jackson.* Harper & Row, 1976.

*The Revolutionary War: America's Fight for Freedom.* National Geographic Society Special Publications Division, 1967.

# The Campaigns of Andrew Jackson During the War of 1812

Here is an activity which will help you to understand the campaigns fought by Andrew Jackson against the Creek Indians and the British from 1813 to 1815. First, draw a circle around the area where the Creek War was fought. On March 24, 1814, Jackson defeated the Indians at Horseshoe Bend. Starting there, draw an arrow to Pensacola, Florida, the site of his battle against the British blockaders. After this victorious battle, Jackson was made a major-general. Next, draw an arrow to New Orleans, Louisiana, where Jackson fought the famous battle against a British invasion in January 1815. As that battle was raging, a treaty between the United States and Great Britain was being signed, but because that was happening so far away, the armies did not know about it and continued fighting. Jackson won this battle and then marched into Florida. Draw an arrow there.

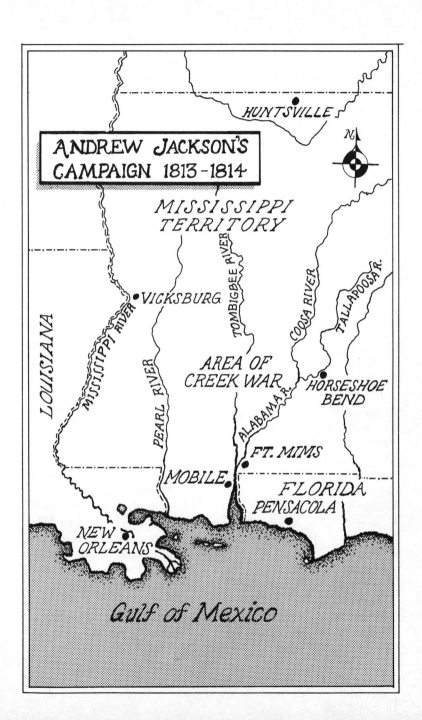

ANDREW JACKSON'S
CAMPAIGN 1813-1814

N

HUNTSVILLE

MISSISSIPPI
TERRITORY

LOUISIANA

MISSISSIPPI RIVER

VICKSBURG

PEARL RIVER

TOMBIGBEE RIVER

COOSA RIVER

TALLAPOOSA R.

AREA OF
CREEK WAR

ALABAMA R.

HORSESHOE
BEND

FT. MIMS

MOBILE

FLORIDA
PENSACOLA

NEW
ORLEANS

Gulf of Mexico

Adams, John Quincy, 124, 135–136, 137, 138, 148
Baratarians, 114
Benton, Thomas Hart, 93–96, 134, 150, 161
Blount, Governor, 91
Boston Harbor, 18–20
Boston Massacre, 17, 161
Boston Tea Party, 18
Calhoun, John C., 90, 146, 149–150, 161
Carrickfergus, 6
Charles Town, 13, 14, 20–21, 23
Cherokee Indians, 71, 77–78
Clay, Henry, 90, 135–136, 153
Coffee, John, 97, 101
Concord, 19
Crawford, James, (uncle), 8– 9, 28
Crawford, Robert (uncle), 20– 21, 23
Creek Indians, 97, 101–106, 109–110
Crockett, Davy, 101
Cumberland Road, 55–56
Davie, William, 25–26
Dickinson, Charles, 83–87
Donelson, Emily, 145, 147, 155
Donelson, Jack, 145
Donelson, John, 58–59, 62
Eaton, John Henry, 130, 137, 147–148
Federalists, 130–131
First Continental Congress, 18
Florida, 123–125, 128–129
Fort Mims, 97, 100, 102
Francis Cummins Boarding School, 15
Gage, Thomas, 18–20
George III, 17, 18
*Globe, The*, 146
Hermitage, 80–81, 126–127, 155
Horsehoe Bend, 104–105
Houston, Sam, 155, 159
Hunter's Hill, 75–76, 80–81
Jackson, Andrew
    Early life
        childhood and education, 8, 9–15
        the Revolutionary War, 21–41
        lawyer, 51–54, 57, 61, 63
        marriage to Rachel, 69, 72
        businessman, 73–74, 79, 81
        congressman, 75–78
    Soldier
        Tennessee State Militia, 79, 90–93
        Indian fighter, 97–108
        battle of New Orleans, 114–121
        Florida, 123–125
    Presidency
        election of 1824, 135–136
        election of 1828, 138
        first administration (1829–1833), 146–153
        second administration (1833–1837), 153–155
Jackson, Andrew (father), 6–8
Jackson, Andrew Jr. (son), 52, 89
Jackson, Elizabeth (mother), 6, 8, 37–38, 40–41

Jackson, Hugh (brother), 23
Jackson, Rachel (wife), 60–61,
64–73, 76, 121–122, 138–141
Jackson, Robert (brother), 25–
26, 30, 38–39
Jarret, Nancy, 51–52
Jay Treaty, 77
Jefferson, Thomas, 90,
131–132
Jonesborough, 55
Lafitte, Jean, 114
Lexington, 19
Lincoyer, 102, 138
Macay, Spruce, 50–52
Madison, James, 90
McNairy, John, 54–57, 61
Minutemen, 18–19
Mobile Bay, 97
Monroe, James, 123–124, 127,
128, 131
Nashville, 55–57, 62
Natchez, 63, 69–70
Old Hickory, 93
Overton, John, 58, 60, 72
Patriots, 18, 19
Red Eagle, 97, 99–100,
103–104, 106–108

Republican Party, 131
Robards, Lewis, 60–61,
64–67, 72, 137
Salisbury, 49–50
Sevier, "Nolichucky" Jack,
26–27, 75, 164
Stone Ferry, 23
Stokes, John, 52–53
Sumter, Thomas, 23, 24–25,
26
Tecumseh, 99–100
Tennessee, 74, 75
Texas, 155, 159
Tories, 18
Townshend Acts, 16–17
Truxton, 81–83
Tyler, John, 159
United States Bank, 153–154
Van Buren, Martin, 137, 146,
153, 155
War of 1812, 90, 111–121
Washington, George, 77
Waxhaw Militia Company,
20–23
Waxhaws, 7–10, 22, 24–31
Weatherford, William, *See*
Red Eagle